Textile

EDITED BY
PENNINA BARNETT,
JANIS JEFFERIES
AND DORAN ROSS

THE JOURNAL OF
CLOTH AND CULTURE

VOLUME 1
ISSUE 1
SPRING 2003

ORDERING INFORMATION
Three issues per volume. One volume per annum.
2003: Volume 1

ONLINE
www.bergpublishers.com

BY MAIL
Berg Publishers
C/O Turpin Distribution (Customer Services Dept)
Blackhorse Road
Letchworth
Herts SG6 1HN
UK

BY FAX
+ 44 (0)1462 483011

BY TELEPHONE
+ 44 (0)1462 672555

FOR ENQUIRIES
email: subscriptions@turpinltd.com

ENQUIRIES
Editorial: Kathryn Earle, Managing Editor,
email kearle@berg1.demon.co.uk

Production: Sara Everett, Director
email severett@bergpublishers.com

Advertising: Joanne Hutt,
email jhutt@bergpublishers.com

SUBSCRIPTION DETAILS
Free Online Subscription for Print Subscribers.

Full color images available online.

Access your electronic subscription through
www.ingenta.com or www.ingentaselect.com

Institutional base list subscription price:
US$160.00, £100.00

Individuals' subscription price: US$65.00, £40.00

Berg Publishers is the imprint of
Oxford International Publishers Ltd.

EDITORS
Pennina Barnett and **Janis Jefferies**
UK, Goldsmiths College

Doran Ross
UCLA Fowler Museum of Cultural History

Book Reviews Editor:
Please send all books for consideration for review in *Textile* to:
Victoria Mitchell
Norwich School of Art & Design, St George Street, Norwich,
NR3 1BB, UK
victoria@nsad.ac.uk

Exhibition Reviews Editors:
UK and Rest of World:
Jennifer Harris, The Whitworth Art Gallery, University of
Manchester, Whitworth Park, Manchester, M15 6ER, UK
jennifer.harris@man.ac.uk

USA
Rebecca Stevens
Contemporary Textiles, The Textile Museum, 23250 S Street
NW, Washington DC 20008-4088, USA
stevensgrj@aol.com

AIMS AND SCOPE
Cloth accesses an astonishingly broad range of human experiences. The raw material from which things are made, it has various associations: sensual, somatic, decorative, functional and ritual. Yet although textiles are part of our everyday lives, their very familiarity and accessibility belie a complex set of histories, and invite a range of speculations about their personal, social and cultural meanings. This ability to move within and reference multiple sites gives textiles their potency.

This journal brings together research in textiles in an innovative and distinctive academic forum for all those who share a multifaceted view of textiles within an expanded field. Representing a dynamic and wide-ranging set of critical practices, it provides a platform for points of departure between art and craft; gender and identity; cloth, body and architecture; labor and technology; techno-design and practice – all situated within the broader contexts of material and visual culture.

Textile invites submissions informed by technology and visual media, history and cultural theory; anthropology; philosophy; political economy and psychoanalysis. It draws on a range of artistic practices, studio and digital work, manufacture and object production.

SUBMISSIONS
Should you have a topic you would like us to consider, please send an abstract of 300–500 words to one of the editors. Notes for Contributors can be found at the back of the journal and style guidelines are available by emailing fhowlett@bergpublishers.com or from the Berg website (www.bergpublishers.com).

ISSN: 1475-9756
www.bergpublishers.com

Contents

EDITORS

Pennina Barnett and **Janis Jefferies**
Department of Visual Arts
Goldsmiths College
New Cross
London
SE14 6NW
UK
p.barnett@gold.ac.uk
j.jefferies@gold.ac.uk

Doran Ross
UCLA
Fowler Museum of Cultural History
308 Charles Young Drive
Los Angeles CA 90095-1549
USA

doran@isop.ucla.edu

Letter from the Editors

Welcome to the first issue of *Textile: The Journal of Cloth and Culture*.

"Textile" means different things to different people, and this is exactly what our new journal aims to address. Rather than dwelling on definitions and territories, we want to encourage debate—and argument—across disciplines, borders, and cultures, by bringing together cutting-edge research in an innovative and distinctive international academic forum.

Textile will embrace a dynamic and wide-ranging set of critical practices, from visual and material culture—studio and digital work, manufacture, and object production—to cultural theory, political economy, philosophy, anthropology, and psychoanalysis. In sum, we advocate a multifaceted view of textiles within an expanded field. As far as we are aware, no existing journal on textiles has such an ambitious remit. Yet we believe *Textile* to be very much of the moment: research across different academic fields has been converging for some time, as scholars "borrow" theoretical discourses and approaches from each other. The launch of this journal offers the occasion to reflect upon some of the ideas, theories, and developments that have been influential in relation to discussions of cloth. What follows is by no means comprehensive, but is, at least, a place to start a debate.

The idea of "an expanded field" is borrowed from the well-known essay by American art historian Rosalind Krauss called "Sculpture in the Expanded Field."[1] Writing in 1979, Krauss was looking back at a decade of developments that seemed to test the very category of sculpture: piles of thread wasted on the floor, narrow corridors with TV monitors at the ends, temporary lines cut into the floor of the desert.[2] She argued that the category had been "forced to cover such a heterogeneity that it [was], itself, in danger of collapsing," for as ". . . we stare at the pit in the earth and think we both do and don't know what sculpture is." Her essay evolves into a complex analysis, but her opening remarks have resonances for textiles, in particular what has variously been called avant-garde textiles, art textiles, textile or fiber art—a lack of consensus which demonstrates the difficulty and "edginess" of describing a practice that seems to fall between genres.[3] For as with sculpture, the category "textile" has, as Krauss put it, been "kneaded and stretched and

Textile, Volume 1, Issue 1, pp. 1–7
Reprints available directly from the Publishers.
Photocopying permitted by licence only.

twisted in an extraordinary demonstration of elasticity, a display of the way in which a cultural term can be extended to include just about anything."

The 1960s and 1970s are often cited as critical moments in the development of textiles practice, a period when many artists, particularly in Europe, Japan, and the United States, started to question and subvert textile techniques and traditions, and like their counterparts in sculpture, explore the formal qualities of materials and processes as ends in themselves. Many experimented with film, photography, performance, and dance. Others engaged with cultural theories and practices such as feminism, psychoanalysis, semiology, structuralism, poststructuralism, modernism, and postmodernism. As a result of these encounters, textiles, it could be argued, has come of age as a critical and self-reflexive practice. Yet there are still those who ask what "all this theory" is for. Theories simply offer ways to think about things, to consider ideas, or question the underlying assumptions of "common sense." And increasingly, the process is two way. For just as artists, designers, scholars, curators, and others concerned with cloth have looked outward, so those involved in fine art, literature, philosophy, and many other areas have recognized the potential of cloth. An example is the work of Rozsika Parker, who trained as an art historian, and was one of the founding members of the pioneering feminist magazine of the 1970s, *Spare Rib*. In an early issue of the magazine she wrote an article called "The Word for Embroidery was Work," in which she asked why what had once been a prestigious art, practiced by both men and women in the Middle Ages, came, by the nineteenth century, to be devalued as a feminine craft and leisure activity, practiced by upper-class women. In researching the history of embroidery, Parker traced another history: the social history of women, and the shifting notions of femininity and roles ascribed to them. The result was her ground-breaking book *The Subversive Stitch: Embroidery and the Making of the Feminine*.[4]

A Good Organum of Fabric

Interdisciplinarity is increasingly regarded as essential critical practice, for a discipline that builds walls around itself, just like a country that becomes a fortress, is likely to stagnate. Here the philosopher Michel Serres offers a pertinent image:

> *I believe that there is box-thought, the thought we call rigorous,*
> *like rigid, inflexible boxes, and sack-thought, like systems of fabric.*
> *Our philosophy lacks a good organum of fabrics.*[5]

The dictionary defines cloth as a "soft, usually pliable fabric."[6] Serres also argues for "soft logics"—modes of thought that are open and inclusive. *Textile* aims to encourage new ways of thinking about cloth that resemble this soft, loose weave.

The metaphors of cloth, its weave and texture, have proved a rich source for many philosophers.

In recent years, Deleuzian ideas, in particular, have attracted the attention of cultural critics, architects, and those engaged with visual culture. In *The Fold: Leibniz and the Baroque*, Deleuze retraces the steps of the seventeenth-century German philosopher.[7] He describes "the fold that goes out to infinity," as endlessly composing and recomposing, without inside or outside, beginning or end; a movement in which disparate elements encounter and separate, producing new modes of thought. Here, "thinking" is not something we automatically do, or a knowledge we already have, but immanent, creative, experimental, and critical.[8] Within the dizzying Deleuzian universe, folds abound: in the fantastic curves of the Baroque, its swathing draperies and billowing clothes; the curling fruits and vegetables of its still-life paintings; in wind and water; in sound, as it moves through the air; in the layers of sediment that make up the earth; in the flux and flow of matter; and in our own complicated selves (*complicare*, Latin: "to fold together;" *plier*, French: "to fold"). Indeed, the world itself becomes a body of infinite folds and surfaces, moving through compressed time and space.

The Economy/ies of Touch

Twisting and turning in the Deleuzian universe, what might happen when, for example, visual culture encounters anthropology or linguistics meets techno-theory? A linguist might take us on an etymological journey around the word cloth, emphasizing its tangible qualities: *tangere*, Latin: "to touch, reach, arrive at." The word cloth appears to originate from the Germanic *kleid*, dress or garment, *kleidung*, clothing, and the Dutch *kleed*. It is thought to come from the root *kli-*, "to stick or cling to," which makes cloth: "that which clings to the body."[9] And because our bodies are always in contact with cloth, it has sensory and suggestive powers, which can stir both conscious and unconscious memory.

Anthropologists remind us that we are constructed by our senses. Within some cultures, smell is privileged; in others tactility. Yet even within the realm of touch, the meaning and value attributed to qualities of surface can vary: in one smoothness may be valued, in another roughness. Furthermore, spatial relations vary within these sensory economies. For when it comes to sight, we can observe from a distance. But inherent to touch is the idea of proximity, making it, perhaps, one of the most intimate of the senses. For while it is possible to see without being seen,[10] ". . . to touch is always to be touched . . ."[11] Through the play of language, at least in English, this takes an emotional turn: for to be touched involves a capacity to be moved or affected, for we can never emerge (fully) intact from any encounter (*intact*-[*us*], Latin: "untouched, uninjured, entire, whole, complete;" *afficere*, Latin: "to do something to, to touch, work upon . . . to cause change").

At the time of writing, an exhibition of the work of artist Eva Hesse (1936–1970) is showing in London at Tate Modern. Based predominantly in New York during the 1960s, Hesse experimented with soft materials such as rope and latex, as well as fiber glass. Much of her work is slowly disintegrating. It was not intended to last. Yet standing before her sculptures, questions of permanence, fragility, and materiality arise—as if these emotive, organic, at times "formless" forms reflect back to us our own fragile and embodied subjectivity. For cloth, like the body, is a "mediating surface" through which we encounter the world.

The Ocular-centricity of the West

Focusing on touch challenges the ocular-centricity of Western culture, and its tendency to compartmentalize the senses. The Christo-Hellenic tradition emphasizes enlightenment, insight, revelation, the visionary, implying that knowledge can be seen, and truth sought, in the material world: the Turin Shroud, a weeping statue of the Virgin Mary . . .

The Western empirical tradition privileges observation and experience as the basis of knowledge. Sight has become associated with truth and, by turns, both rational thought and personal opinion. Involuntarily, we say: "I see what you mean;" "from my perspective;" "in my view;" "in my mind's eye;" "I observe that;" "it appears that . . ." In the hierarchy of the senses, the Western tradition, while privileging sight, relegates touch and smell to the lower rungs.[12]

Of course the eye does not just look. The haptic, or visual–tactile, describe experiences that are simultaneously ocular and tactile. Perhaps it is ironic that it is through new media, and in particular digital technologies, that we have been forced to question issues regarding materiality. As Paul Virilio has written: "to feel at a distance, that amounts to shifting the perspective towards a domain it did not encompass: that of contact, of contact at a distance."[13]

The Weaving of Pure Algebra[14]

The relationship between textiles, industrialization, and technology is well established. Yet the Jacquard loom, with its sophisticated punch-card system, led to developments far beyond the world of textile manufacture, which would have been inconceivable to its inventor. As techno-theorist, Sadie Plant relates in her extraordinary book *Zeros + Ones*, Jacquard's work fascinated the engineer Charles Babbage, who for many years had been working on a futuristic calculating machine, the Difference Engine. Babbage was the proud owner of five-foot square portrait of Jacquard, woven at 1,000 silk threads to the inch, and with an extraordinary 24,000 punched-hole cards, each capable of carrying over 1,000 punch holes! Plant describes how the work of Ada, Countess Lovelace (daughter of Lord Byron and his mathematician wife Annabella), came to Babbage's attention. Babbage consequently invited her to join him in his research, and the two went on to work together. What they produced later came to be called to be called "computer programming," a century before the hardware had even been built.[15]

Ada Lovelace could never have envisaged that what had begun with the weaving of elaborate patterned silks—and were transfigured by her own "algebraic weaving"—would, in turn, lead to the:

digital machines of the late twentieth century [that] weave new networks from what were once isolated words, numbers, music, shapes, smells, tactile textures, architectures and countless channels as yet unnamed.[16]

Or that the yarns threaded through Jacquard punch holes would:

twist and turn through the history of computing, technology, the science and arts . . . up and down through the ages of spinning and weaving, back and forth through the fabrication of fabrics, shuttles and looms, cotton and silk, canvas and paper, brushes and pens, typewriters, carriages, telephone wires, synthetic fibers, electrical filaments, silicon strands, fiber-optic cables, pixeled screens, telecom lines, the World Wide Web, the Net, and matrices to come.[17]

Textile and Text

The relationship between text and textile—and their common root: *texere*, "to weave," and *textum*, "a web or texture"—has been much cited in critical writings about cloth. The work of Roland Barthes has been particularly influential. Barthes describes the text as a "woven fabric," made up of a "weave of signifiers," "a tissue of quotations drawn from the innumerable centres of culture."[18] The implication is that all writing— all creative activity—can be located within wider systems of reference: a network of ideas across time and space. Rather than thinking of the text (which could be a book, but equally a piece of cloth, a film, or even a city) as something finite, a thread from the author to the reader, Barthes sees it as open ended. The reader, no longer a passive receiver of meanings, is also a producer of meanings within his or her own right, and joins the author as a weaver of texts. This is precisely what Plant demonstrates in her discussion of the work of Ada Lovelace. For although Lovelace began by annotating a text by the Italian military engineer Louis Menabrea, she proceeded to make links across it, producing something new in her own right. The age of the computer, of hypertext and the world wide web, make the metaphor of the text ever more pertinent. For as Plant has pointed out, "hypertext programmes and the net are webs of footnotes without central points, organising principles, (or) hierarchies."[19]

Yet this now well-rehearsed idea of the text as the play and production of meaning—open, provisional, plural—has ancient roots. For in the Talmudic tradition, scholars did not seek revelation. Instead they understood that each text opens up another, deriving from, yet different from its source, generating and creating further writing, reading, and interpretation, *ad infinitum*.

Collecting Cloth

This idea of the text has informed scholarship in diverse ways. Recounting a debate amongst museum workers, anthropologist Daniel Miller shows how the concept of the text cuts across received ideas of classification.[20] The museum curators cannot work out where a particular set of chintz designs, known as the "Oriental style," originate. After some research, they decide that the style comes from India, yet cannot strictly be classified as Indian. Miller explains that when Indian cloth was first exported to Europe, the British wanted neither copies of their own textile designs, nor those indigenous to India itself. They wanted, instead, something that fitted their image of what the Indians should have been making for themselves: exotic, but "tasteful." After a series of to-ings and fro-ings over great distances, a satisfactory design was eventually produced. Although produced in India, the Oriental style is not an "authentic" Indian design. Nor is it British. Rather, it is "a design which has meaning only as an expression of the relationship between two societies . . ." Miller compares the initial cycle of designs to Laing's "what I think you think I think," in that they mediated between each society's image of the other, taking on a certain autonomy, and becoming "an increasingly fixed material text . . . until eventually we are left with discussion not of British–Indian relations, but merely of the oriental style of the cloth in itself." (See Lemire in this issue for further related discussion.)

The 1990s saw a revival of interest in ethnic crafts within the West. Yet if we look at the history of oriental carpets, for example, we see that the West has had a long-standing fascination with such artifacts. Indeed, anthropologist Brian Spooner created an interesting term to describe the Western fascination with oriental carpets: ruggism.[21] An off-shoot of orientalism (and therefore related to the Western Romantic tradition), ruggism is characterized by a disenchantment with Western industrialized society and a yearning for pre-modern ways of life. This is a configuration of the myth of the noble savage, here imagined as living a more cohesive or wholesome lifestyle, and producing "meaningful artifacts that have both symbolic and social significance. Yet if we look at the history of the production and commodification of oriental carpets, we see that they too are texts: of a long history of trade, industrialization, colonization, and cultural relations.

In touching upon some of these ideas, we trust that the fantastic potential of the journal is evident. We do not have a preset agenda but instead hope that *Textile* will provide a platform for discussion of, for example, art and craft; gender and identity; cloth, body, and architecture; postcolonial theory, labor, and technology; techno-design and practice; and ideas and fields yet to be imagined. Appropriately, contributors to this inaugural issue approach cloth from diverse perspectives.

For Anne Hamlyn, fabric is both a fetishized and fetishizing surface. Her article takes as its starting point Sigmund Freud's definition of sexual fetishism to explore "the politically uncomfortable associations between women, fetishism and cloth." Through examples from fine art and cinema, she asks whether it is possible to be seduced by the tactile play of surfaces of the kind that fabric sets up, yet to remain critically incisive.

Jenni Sorkin critically appraises the pioneering work and contribution of North American writer and curator Mildred Constantine, who in 1969, together with textile designer Jack Lenor Larsen, curated the ground-breaking *Wall Hangings* at MOMA in New York. This major international exhibition included the work of artists such as Ed Rossbach, Olga de Amaral, Anni Albers, Gunta Stšlzl, Magdalena Abakanowicz, Sheila Hicks, and Lenore Tawney. Together with their collaborative work on two important books (*Beyond Craft: The Art Fabric Mainstream* (1973) and *The Art Fabric: Mainstream* (1981)), the exhibition was formative in establishing the work of textile or fiber artists.

Steve Connor asks why it is so difficult to wear clothing or have furnishings with spotted patterns. His paper considers the signification of spots, dots, blotches, and patches within the social and cultural history of Western Europe. It examines the association of spots with disease, stigmatization, and disorder—describing for example, how Jews in medieval Europe were required to wear a colored roundel of cloth—yet also the ways in which spots have been associated with beauty, as the curious fashion amongst seventeenth-century women of adding patches and black "beauty" spots to the face demonstrates.

Beverly Lemire's paper locates textile production at the heart of global trading history. She traces how the painted and printed Indian cottons imported to Europe by the East India Company came to transform English domestic interiors. She argues that, although at first their floral patterns evoked the "exotic" landscapes from which they came, by the eighteenth century these bolts of printed floral fabric not only came to epitomize the strengths of industrial Britain, but were appropriated to signify Englishness.

The discursive nature of the journal relies on current research taking place across the globe. In particular, we welcome papers from outside the Europe–US–Australia triangle. We actively seek proposals for papers, so get writing! For the journal aspires to be "a good organum of fabric," in which writers and readers join together as weavers of texts; where new modes of "soft" thought flourish; and complex ideas take shape (*complexum . . . complecti*, Latin: "to fold or twine together;" *plectere*: "to plait, interweave, twist"). In sum, we hope *Textile* will become a web or network across space and time, which generates and creates further writing, reading, and interpretation.

Finally, we would like to thank all those who have worked with us to shape and produce the journal. As well as those who have contributed papers and reviews to this first issue, there are many people behind the scenes: colleagues who have refereed papers; Exhibitions and Book Reviews Editors Jennifer Harris, Victoria Mitchell, and Rebecca Stevens; the International Editorial Board; Celeste Stroll, *Textile* Administrator; and a special thanks to the team at Berg Publishers in Oxford.

Pennina Barnett
on behalf of co-editors
Janis Jefferies and Doran Ross

Notes

1. Rosalind, Krauss, 1979, "Sculpture in the Expanded Field," in Hal Foster (ed.), *Postmodern Culture*, Pluto Press, London and Sydney, 1983.
2. Krauss was referring to artists such as Robert Morris, Robert Smithson, and Richard Long.
3. Sarat Maharaj, "Textile Art—Who Are You?, Distant Lives/Shared Voices," commissioned essay for an International Art Project, Lodz, 1992.
4. Roszika Parker, *The Subversive Stitch: Embroidery and the Making of the Feminine*, The Women's Press, London, 1984. Parker's discussion focused on the European context, and predominantly on British embroidery.
5. Michel Serres, *Rome, The Book of Foundations* (1983), trans. Felicia McCarren, Stanford University Press, Stanford, CA, 1991, p. 236.
6. *The Universal Dictionary of the English Language*, Henry Cecil Wyld (ed.), Routledge & Kegan Paul, London, 1952.
7. Gilles Deleuze, *The Fold: Leibniz and the Baroque* (1988), trans. Tom Conley, Athlone Press, London, 1993.
8. Ibid., p. 121.
9. Ewa Kuryluk, *Veronica and Her Cloth: History, Symbolism, and Structure of a "True" Image*, Basil Blackwell, Cambridge, MA, and Oxford, UK, 1991, p. 179.
10. Denis Hollier, *The Politics of Prose: Essay on Sartre* [1986], cited in Joan Livingstone and Anne Wilson, "The Presence of Touch," in *The Presence of Touch* (exhibition catalog), Department of Fiber, The School of the Art Institute of Chicago, Chicago, IL, 1996, p. 6.
11. Paul Rodaway, *Sensuous Geographies: Body, Sense and Place* [1994], cited in Joan Livingstone and Anne Wilson, ibid., p. 1.
12. I am indebted here to David Howes, Concordia University, Canada and Georgina Kleege, novelist and author. Many of the ideas about touch and sight were "imbibed" from their presentations at the first of the ESRC seminars, "Ocularcentricity in the Museum," held at Tate Modern, London, 1 November 2002, and organized by Fiona Candlin, Birkbeck College, University of London/British Museum, and Caro Howell, Tate Modern.
13. Paul Virilio, "Speed and Information: Cyberspace Alarm!" www. aec.al/c/theory. (Thanks to Alicia Felberbaum for this reference).
14. William Gibson and Bruce Sterling, *The Difference Machine*, cited in Sadie Plant, *Zeros + Ones, Digital Women + The New Technoculture*, Fourth Estate, London, 1997, paperback edition 1998, p. 23.
15. Ibid., p. 9.
16. Ibid., pp. 11–12.
17. Ibid., p. 12.
18. Roland Barthes, "The Death of the Author," in *Image Music Text*, Fontana Press, London, 1977, p. 146.
19. Sadie Plant, *Zeros + Ones*, p. 10.
20. Daniel Miller, "Primitive Art and the Necessity of Primitivism to Art" in Susan Hiller (ed.), *The Myth of Primitivism: Perspectives on Art*, Routledge, London, 1991, pp. 58–60.
21. Brian Spooner, "Weavers and Dealers: The Authenticity of an Oriental Carpet," in Arjun Appadurai (ed.), *The Social Life of Things: Commodities in Cultural Perspective*, Cambridge University Press, Cambridge, 1988 edn. See also Pennina Barnett, "Rugs R Us (And Them): The Oriental Carpet as Sign and Text," *Third Text* 30, Spring 1995, pp. 13–28.

Freud, Fabric, Fetish

Abstract

"**F**reud, Fabric, Fetish" explores the nature of the relation between women and cloth in everyday life, visual culture and psychoanalytic theory. The article proposes that the sensory connection that we all (both male and female) have to cloth cannot be adequately expressed in language. This, it is argued in psychoanalytic terms, is because the unique "language" of fabric straddles the pre-linguistic or Imaginary and the social/linguistic codes that make up the Symbolic order. Fabric is, further, shown to complicate assumptions about sexual difference because it is inevitably caught up in the persistent undecidability of the fetishistic fantasy. This uncertainty in the fabric-as-fetish becomes evident in selected examples from film and the visual arts.

ANNE HAMLYN

Anne Hamlyn is a writer and lecturer. She has taught and written on a wide variety of subjects including psychoanalysis, cinema, textiles and performance art. She has recently completed her Ph.D. on the subject of temporality and 1960s visual culture and is currently preparing it for publication.

Textile, Volume 1, Issue 1, pp. 9–27
Reprints available directly from the Publishers.
Photocopying permitted by licence only.

Freud, Fabric, Fetish

The film theorist Christian Metz reminds us that "A fetish is always material: in so far as one can make up for it by the power of the symbolic alone one is precisely no longer a fetishist."[1] I run the risk of exploiting a rather obvious pun on the word "material" here but, in this context, the etymological coincidence is not without significance. Without attempting to be exhaustive, this article will tie together some of the cultural discourses around the fetish and, at the same time, bring this excessively over-invested theoretical terrain back to the "matter at hand," that is to say *fabric*. This may go some way towards resolving the politically (with a small "p") uncomfortable associations between women and fetishism and cloth. I am not the first writer to have considered the fetish and textiles from the point of view of gender; however, the connection between them seems as yet unresolved. I will, therefore, return to Sigmund Freud's original definitions of sexual fetishism as one way of considering afresh the cultural significance of the textile.

The Theoretical Fetishist

In one of Sigmund Freud's earliest discussions of fetishism, a paper given to the Vienna Psychoanalytic Society in 1909, he described the case history of a male clothes fetishist for whom "all interest in women [was] displaced onto clothes" and whose symptoms during analysis included the "conspicuous [. . .] adjust[ing of] the creases of his trousers."[2] He was, according to Freud, "physically impotent, and despite his numerous affairs, had never successfully completed coitus."[3] The analyst describes how:

Once, for example, he awaited a rendezvous with the lady who was his sweetheart: but his feelings of love immediately vanished when she appeared in poor clothes which had been thrown on hurriedly. It also turned out that his sudden fallings-out during later love affairs always originated in the fact that he objected to a piece of her clothing.[4]

While it may (or may not) be surprising that a man should be so thoroughly invested in such a superficial matter as women's clothing, what is the more remarkable about Freud's characterization of the fetishist is the man's less private idiosyncrasies:

In this patient something similar to what took place in the erotic domain occurred in the intellectual domain: he turned his interest away from things onto words which are, so to speak, the clothes of ideas; this accounts for his interest in philosophy.[5]

In this case history a very useful parallel is being set up between a pathological and seemingly bizarre relation to cloth (or rather its derivations) and a relatively normal and acceptable (if not always comprehensible) passion for critical analysis. Freud's patient is a theorist!

At the start of this discussion Freud's case history leads one to question how one form of passion— the passion for critical analysis— can comprehend the other—the passion for surfaces? It is often assumed, in cultural theory in general, that one cannot be both seduced by the tactile play of surfaces of the kind that fabric sets up and critically incisive at the same time. In critical/academic circles, it seems, you either occupy the world of knowledge and insight, commanding language and representation, both of which are grounded in the psychic register that Lacan calls the *Symbolic*, or you are fated to remain embedded in the seductive world of the sensual, distracted by surfaces and illusions, a narcissistic mode of experience that Lacan associates with the *Imaginary*.

I will go on to describe how fabric subversively occupies either or both of the two seemingly incompatible fields of "interest" laid out by Freud in his case history of the male clothes fetishist: that of (Imaginary) seduction by the surface issue of women's clothes and the (Symbolic) distance of the theorizing process. These two modes of response to the world (we might, for simplicity's sake, call them *touching* and *naming*) can be set up in critical relation to each other and this form of criticality is something that I will be staging here. I would like to suggest that much theory has conspicuously failed to address the relationship

between these two positions because doing so might disclose some nasty "little secrets." As I will go on to suggest, the *secret* at issue here is the perpetually unresolved "problem" (as Freud had put it) of the female body and its desires.

With the help of visual examples from fine art and cinema, I will argue that the one process, naming, *can* comprehend the other, touching, but only once considered from the, so-called, feminine point of view. I do not, however, wish to proscribe who (male or female) may take on that point of view at any one time, but I will suggest that women, in their seeming social, sexual, and economic "intimacy" with fabric-as-fetish, *may* , if they choose, occupy that ambiguous position for critical ends. Hence, my discussions will emphasize that, for the fetishist, the woman's body is only *half hidden* and, as such, there is always the potential space for its own desires to make themselves felt. For the surface (the material attire in which the clothes fetishist so heartily invests) is also the ground for the expression of the woman's *own* psychic investments. This is something that the fetishist (any fetishist) necessarily fails to register. Here Freud's analysand falls in line with the traditional point of view of theory. That is to say, *his* objections to his lady friend's "attire" may appear loud and urgent but *her* objections to being told in what acceptable guise she should appear may be just as pressing.

Fabric as it Undoes Itself

Fabric acts to conceal and cover objects and persons while, at the same time, disclosing them— hinting at their presence. Man Ray's

photograph *The Riddle* or *The Enigma of Isadore Ducasse* (1920) illustrates fabric's constitutional ambiguity: a vaguely recognizable object, or group of objects, is enveloped in a rough textile and tied up with a rope. The objects may be commonplace but the wrapping gives them a certain mystery, vitality, and seductiveness. Fabric is malleable. It lends itself to wrapping, draping, and swathing. It restricts direct access to the naked object, but it also has the ability to suggest, enhance, and draw attention to what it covers over and adorns.

Like a sumptuous textile, cinema has been seen as a seductive, fetishized and fetishizing, surface that both is, and is not, what it represents or enfolds. Christian Metz's application of the idea of fetishism to cinema is useful for textiles because it raises three closely related discourses, all of which are appropriate to fabric: those of desire, of gender, and of the surface. Metz's suggestion was that cinema conceals and discloses the absence of its referent and this emptiness, or lack, in the medium is fetishistically suspended by the absorbing nature of the surface images and the narratives they construct. Throughout its history popular cinema has tended to be perceived by its critics as rendering its consumer/audience passive, feminized, even mute in the face of its sensory immediacy.[6] The audience is seen as incapable of critical judgment because, we might say, they cannot *theorize* their object adequately. Such interpretations set up a distinct hierarchy of value in which truth, authenticity and knowledge (social,

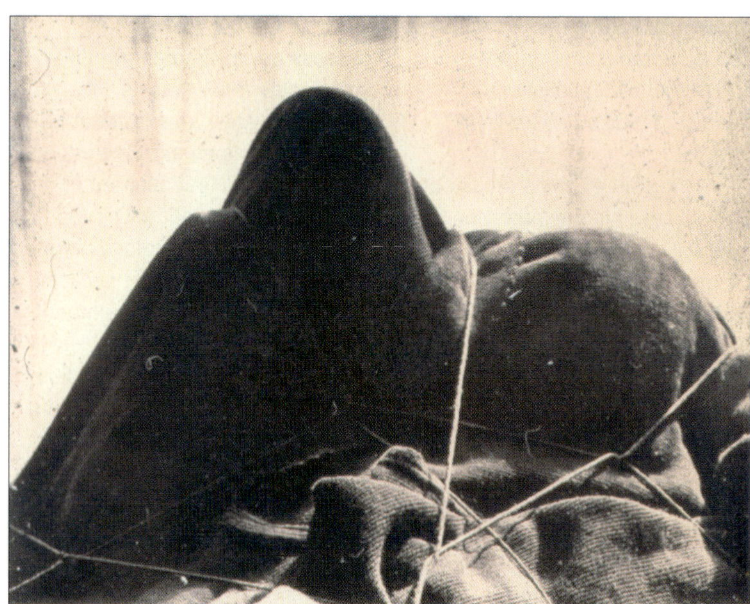

Figure 1
Man Ray, "The Enigma of Isadore
Ducasse" (1920). Copyright courtesy of
The Man Ray Trust/ADAGP, Paris and
DACS London 2002.

economic, moral etc.) are seen as structures that are hidden by the surface, and the surface is further seen as something potentially (if not always) compromised and compromising.

In considering another discourse in which the discursive relationship between surface and depth, façade and structure has been of crucial importance—that of post-modernist architecture—Mark Wigley comments on how the seduction of surfaces:

> *[. . .] is set up in opposition to theory: the theorist is the one who is able to resist seduction. The rejection of surface effects, like the whole tradition of such rejections around which the Western tradition of theory has organized itself, is tacitly understood as the control of sexual desire.*[7]

The fetish is "tacitly" understood as something compulsive, an unthinking and self-indulgent erotic and/or atavistic foible associated with the unmastered body and the so-called primitive.[8] In film criticism, a film viewer who is passive and seduced by the technology or material elements of the projection is generally figured "in the feminine." The theorist, critic or avant-garde director on the other hand, the one who detaches him/herself from such surfaces, attacking what David Harvey calls the "malleability of appearances" and activating language to penetrate their hidden depths (or expose a lack thereof) is more often described as masculine: authoritative and phallic.[9] I would like to suggest that the refusal of seduction bares an unmistakable resemblance to the rejection of textiles as a significant art practice by those in positions of power and authority on the basis of its associations with the decorative and, of course, with femininity.[10]

A Twofold Fetishism

I will give an example of the interpretative dilemma that such epistemologies create by setting out a scene from Martin Scorsese's sumptuous adaptation of Edith Wharton's novel *The Age of Innocence* (1993) and allowing my further analyses to develop from it.[11]

Escaping from heavy snowfall on a busy city street the couple step into a covered carriage. He wears a caped overcoat and she is bustled and corseted in a fur-trimmed overdress. The interior of the carriage has walls of thick padded silk that force the pair into unaccustomed proximity. For a moment they sit awkwardly. After a pause he pronounces uncertainly, "Each time I see you you happen to me all over again." She smiles, abashed but gratified. "Yes I know, for me too," she places her gloved hand affectionately on top of his. He contemplates her hand momentarily and then, removing his own larger and coarser leather glove, turns it upwards to reveal the several bright pearl buttons that join the soft suede at the wrist. He slowly unfastens them to expose her pale skin. Prising apart the two halves of the opening he lifts the underside of her wrist to his lips. She watches him intently and then, overwhelmed, embraces him. The horses whinny as the carriage jerks forward and pulls away.

The meaning and effect of the scene described relies not so much on action nor even on dialogue, but on the use of fabric and furnishings to encourage a form of sensuous voyeurism in the audience: non-verbal (optical, oral, tactile) elements of the *mise en scène* combine to put across a feeling of stolen intimacy and heightened emotion. It does not take training in psychoanalytic terminology and techniques for this textile language to be understood and enjoyed. In the compressed and quilted space of the carriage, beneath the overcoats and corsetry, the limits of social and sexual decorum are being severely tested. In the scene described, and in *The Age of Innocence* as a whole, the material *stuff*—mounds of it—that is piled over the desiring bodies of the actor/protagonists evokes a fierce repression: desire is hemmed in and "stitched up" by overbearing external pressure, restrained, enfolded, and *bound* in its excessive material environment. It is by virtue of the weight of fabric that the emotional charge of the unbuttoning of the glove stands out so powerfully.

The glove is a classic figure for the fetish and the focal point of all the fetishisms expressed in the sequence. Here, as in the original novel, Madame Olenska's dainty garment is figured poignantly as something of exaggerated preciousness: it is for Newland "as if he had kissed a relic."[12] It is, therefore, not the desired object that he lifts to his lips but something else, something *like it*, something that *stands in close contact with it*, something nearly but, crucially, not quite *it* but that is nonetheless an object of extraordinary power and reverence. We see, here, how the fetish treads a tightrope as the focus of desire for it encloses, but at the same time discloses, the presence of the *real* object of curiosity and desire. However, if the object of immediate attention comes too close to that "other" object the fetishism fails and desire is suddenly unbound. It is as if the fetishized surface (here the fabric of the glove) undoes itself and that undoing unleashes a potentially dangerous overspill of free-wheeling desire. Desire needs to be bound to something in order to be potentially satisfied, in other words, in order for there to be pleasure. *Too much* pleasure can itself be destabilizing and, in psychoanalytic terms, desire unbound *is anxiety*.

It is, therefore, interesting to speculate as to who shows the greater amount of fetishism, the protagonists *in the scene* or the viewer (myself) indulging in the upholstery of the romance. Both fabric and cinema (and in particular the cinema of historical romance) are products that have, culturally speaking, a highly gendered orientation to their consumers. Costume dramas are seen as the penchant of women and, I confess, there is a delicious form of pleasure to be derived from Bonnet Dramas and Bodice Rippers—a somewhat guilty pleasure given my own claims to a critical intellectualism.[13] Such is my seduction that, as I describe it, the scene smacks of romantic *cliché*; however, when seen within the film narrative this is a moment of intense erotic *frisson*. For strategic purposes, I will not attempt to disentangle myself from the tactile immediacy of the scenario. To be seduced by the sequence (as the countess gives herself up, *momentarily*, to

Newland's advances) seems, *on the surface*, to have little potential as a critical act. Nonetheless, such criticality *can* be affected from his seduced position if the surfaces at issue are analyzed not as something that conceals some more legitimate structure of meaning but as *the* malleable ground across which highly contentious gender politics is being enacted. Hence, what I *will* attempt to do with this strategic self-feminizing is to draw something critical out of an *apparently* compromising and self-indulgent captivation with the glamour of surfaces. In order to do so I will (perhaps paradoxically) return to Freud's theory of fetishism.

The Freudian Fetish

Freud's well-known psychoanalytic rendering of the onset of fetishism in the child acknowledges the significance of the textile and textile-associated items in its generation. This is because of their natural proximity to the primary object of the child's desire. They are the man-made surfaces that envelop the idealized maternal body. Fabric occupies the interstices between the needy flesh of the infant and the nurturing flesh on which it depends and, as the child develops, such textile coverings naturally inspire curiosity as to what lies beneath their folds and stays.

What lies beneath—the "reality" that fabric brushes up against—is female genital difference. It is the refusal to recognize that difference that, for Freud, lies at the root of fetishism. The first moment of encounter with gender *as difference* is traumatic for the child because, he can only encompass *similarity* in his narcissistic purview. It is significant that in Freud's analysis the traumatized child is assumed to be male. In his reading of fetishism the little girl's relation to the maternal body is more problematic because she is *already similar*. She cannot, therefore, be traumatized in the same way by the sight of the female body. However, for Freud both the male and the female child perceive the lack in the female body as "genital deficiency" and invent an infantile "theory" for its absence—*castration*.[14]

According to Freud, in so-called normal sexual development, the male child will accept the "fact" of castration, relinquish his desire for the phallic mother and, finally, identify with the father. He will thereby leave the narcissistic dyad of mother and child and enter into the triangular Oedipal relation. The Oedipal triad is the microcosm of the social and, for Lacan, the Symbolic realm. The entry into the Symbolic is, therefore, the beginning of adult sexual development. It was Freud's understanding that this "adult" form of sexuality was both genital and heterosexual. However, for the fetishist, the process is halted abruptly because the maternal figure is *still phallic*. The male child has provided the castrated woman with a new or "substitute phallus." He does not, therefore, have to relinquish his former belief that his mother is like him. The fetishist does not jettison his primary narcissism in order to enter the socio/sexual realm of adult (hetero)sexuality because he never fully separates himself from the maternal space.

As Freud describes in his well-known 1927 essay "Fetishism," the fetish is a "compromise formation" that allows the fetishist to believe the evidence of his eyes, on one level, but that also defends him from the wounding potential of what he sees by maintaining the earlier belief alongside the new one. Freud likens this to "the stopping of memory in traumatic amnesia."[15] In other words the fetishist goes back to the moment just before, or the moment after, the traumatic encounter and fills in the absence artificially with a reassuring image—an image that will later become the basis for the fetish object. The objects that the child perceives in that traumatic moment "the foot or shoe" or "pieces of underclothing," are often chosen because they "crystallize [. . .] the last moment in which the woman could still be regarded as phallic."[16] Without the presence of the fetish that knowledge would induce an intolerable anxiety.

It is this space of interplay between the fabric and the flesh of the woman's body, the space of potential revelation, that becomes the fetishized ground of male desires. Edith Wharton's novel presents to the reader the interaction between the woman and fabric under the scrutiny of a desiring and thoroughly fetishizing male gaze:

[. . .] Madame Olenska sat half reclined, her head propped on a hand and her wide sleeve leaving the arm bare to the elbow.

It was usual for ladies who received in the evening to wear what were called 'simple dinner dresses'; a close-fitting armour of whale-boned silk, slightly

open at the neck, with lace ruffles filling in the crack, and tight sleeves with a flounce uncovering just enough wrist to show an Etruscan gold bracelet or a velvet band. But Madame Olenska, heedless of tradition, was attired in a long robe of red velvet bordered about the chin and down the front with glossy black fur. Archer remembered, on his last visit to Paris seeing a portrait by a new painter, Carolus Duran, whose pictures were the sensation of the Salon, in which the lady wore one of these bold sheath-like robes with her chin nestling in fur. There was something perverse and provocative in the notion of fur worn in the evening in a heated drawing room, and in the combination of a muffled throat and bare arms; but the effect was undeniably pleasing.[17]

In the passage we see a displacement of desire onto a detail of the woman's body—the phallic form of the hand and forearm, and the head and neck, framed by the fall of red velvet and fur. The description might be mistaken as having come from Sacher-Masoch's infamous erotic novel *Venus in Furs* but for the fact that this flagrantly erotic visual appraisal is couched in a description of received social/sartorial etiquette.[18] The narrator's message to the reader is that Newland does not know what is happening to him or at least he *prefers not to know*. We might suggest that he fails to *theorize* or name his fetishism because he is so willfully seduced by the distracting nature of the fabric that encloses his desired "object." It is this process of

relinquishing reality in favor of its idealized alternative that Freud describes as *disavowal*. In Octave Mannoni's well-known maxim of the fetishist "I know very well but just the same": on an unconscious level the fetishist *knows* the reality of the situation but his own surrogate reality, the tactile textile surface, is an infinitely preferable alternative.[19]

Freud describes fetishism as a perversion. In fact, in psychoanalysis in general, the process of disavowal, of which it is the symptom, becomes the model form of all other sexual perversions. But for Freud it is only in *men* that one encounters fetishism as a perversion.[20] According to Freud the female child has nothing to fear because she is *already castrated*. *She has nothing to protect.* For Freud (perceived) genital deficiency that is disavowed by the female child is internalized by her and played out on and through her own body—as Lacan writes "It is the woman herself who assumes the role of the fetish."[21] Thus women, in an unresolved encounter with genital difference, become hysterics. The male child, on the other hand, is not so passive. His fetishism is a kind of skewed technology in which he invents a surrogate phallus that he *reaches out for* whenever the issue of gender difference becomes too pressing, that is to say, whenever he runs up against the thorny problem of sex.

Unlike the woman the male fetishist is able, through the mechanism of the fetish, to project the castrating threat away from his body. The woman (any woman) is compromised by her "nearness" to the fetish. The film theorist Mary Anne Doane writes that, in the

Lacanian derivation of the Freudian fetish, "women are deprived of the distance required by language." They, therefore, remain trapped in the Imaginary, captivated in and by their self-image.[22] Nonetheless, according to Lacan and Granoff the fetishist shares something with the woman's entrapment for he is still, on one level, locked in the imaginary or dyadic maternal relation and hence, like the woman, cannot symbolize adequately. He also remains enraptured and seduced by the lure of the image. Lacan and Granoff refer specifically to the mirror image that Lacan had described in his analysis of the "mirror stage" of infantile development.[23] What the description implies is that the woman shares the fetishist's captivation with the image but her investment is doubly compromised because *she is the image*. Women are unable to disembody the fetish because they are "denied the symbolic code."[24] Such possession requires a certain distance—a distance that, according to Lacan, can only be provided by the successful (i.e. masculine) resolution of the castration complex. For Lacan "femininity is closeness, nearness, 'wrapped in its own contiguity'."[25]

This wrapping has obvious ramifications for textiles. In linguistic terms it could be said that the fetishism of fabric is metonymic rather than metaphoric. Textile objects are chosen for their contiguity, that is to say, their nearness to the maternal body rather than because they stand in symbolically for the missing phallus—in the manner of a bottle or a big toe.[26] On the other hand, women's bodies can be *appropriated* by another and used to symbolize the phallus with the aid of fabric in the form of corsets, stilettos and rubber cat-suits. This is the kind of appropriation that is seen in the work of the artist Alan Jones. Laura Mulvey in the excellently titled "Fears, Fantasies and the Male Unconscious or 'You Don't Know what is Happening, Do You, Mr. Jones?'" has drawn attention to the fact that, as an exploration of fetishism, Jones's work says very little about actual women and their desires and rather more about the artist's own anxieties concerning castration and the female body that figures it.[27]

In Jones's works the woman's body is presented as all surface transformed with the help of fabrics into a surrogate phallus. This phallusization is often quite literal and even comic. In *Bare Me* (1972), as Mulvey describes, "[t]he phallic woman, rigid and pointing upwards, holding her breasts erect with her hands, is standing in high heels on a tray-like board balanced on two spheres."[28] A more perfect graphic rendition of the woman as an erect penis would be difficult to achieve. Such an image serves to insure the fetishist against the loss that the woman's body might otherwise signify. The fabric in this and other such images by Jones is tight: leather, rubber or a diaphanous textile (more like cling-film than chiffon). This fabric functions like armor to lift and restrict the spread and fall of female flesh. It follows every curve of the body but, crucially, never actually exposes the "offending" mark of genital difference. Jones re-articulates the female body in phallic terms to the extent that one is not certain whether there is any flesh at all beneath the accumulated surfaces. What we seem to end up with is a strange form of female anatomy constructed entirely out of fabric. Jones's women are not unlike a series of articulated rubber dolls.

Women Consuming Textiles

This problem of women's ambiguous relation both to fetishism and textiles is evident in one of Freud's most infamously misogynous passages from the paper "Femininity" (1933). From such a description it may be seen how in the Freudian canon women's intimate and complex relations to fabric are not seen as fetishistic but a form of "natural" intimacy:

Shame, which is considered to be a feminine characteristic par excellence but is far more a

Figure 2
Alan Jones "Bare Me" (1972). Copyright courtesy of The Gothenburg Museum of Art.

matter of convention than might be supposed, has as its purpose, we believe, concealment of genital deficiency. We are not forgetting that at a later time shame takes on other functions. It seems that women have made few contributions to the discoveries and inventions in the history of civilization, there is however one technique which they may have invented—that of plaiting and weaving. If that is so, we should be tempted to guess at the unconscious motive for the achievement. Nature herself would seem to have given the model which this achievement imitates by causing the growth at maturity of the pubic hair that conceals the genitals. The step that remained to be taken lay in making the threads adhere to one another, while on the body they stick into the skin and are only matted together.[29]

There is further evidence for such a contention that women's relation to fabric is natural and men's perverse in Freud's remarks on the fetish to the Vienna Psychoanalytic society. In commenting on the case history of the philosophizing clothes fetishist, Freud makes this curious but significant aside concerning women and here the relationship is formed through consumption as opposed to production:

In the world of everyday experience, we can observe that half of humanity must be classed among the clothes fetishists. All women, that is, are clothes fetishists. Dress plays a puzzling role in them. It is a question

again of the repression of the same drive [the drive to look] this time however in passive form of allowing oneself to be seen, which is repressed by clothes, and on account of which clothes are raised to a fetish. Only now do we understand why women behave defencelessly against the demands of fashion. For them clothes take the place of parts of the body, and to wear the same clothes means only to be able to show what the others can show, means only that one can find in her everything that one can expect from women, an assurance which the woman can give only in this form.[30]

What is it then that "one can expect from women?" For Freud, the man fetishizes sexually, and women produce textiles to assist the process of concealment and revelation. However, when it comes to a universal language of economic exchange it is women who are seen as the fetishists intoxicated by voluptuous surface effects of the commodity. But theirs is not a perverse action; their fetishism is merely a product of their drive to veil genital deficiency and thereby to make themselves attractive to men. This is the ultimate "assurance" that the fetishism of clothes is believed to provide. Consequently, shopping is as "natural" to the modern woman as the weaving of genital hair was to her primitive counterpart! Their/our intoxication with shopping functions because it allows them (or so they believe) to perform the fetish for men. Within this psycho/economic regime their/our own value as objects of exchange is, for Freud, established.

A sort of mirroring is taking place here, a two-way fetishism via the textile with castration on the one side and industrial manufacture on the other. Both of these are, in different ways, realities that are subject to disavowal.[31] Thus, we may say that both men and women's relationship with fabric is informed by *both the unconscious and capitalist exchange*. In fact the boundaries between psyche and economics are blurred when it comes to fabric. Fabric is the ground of some of our earliest subject/object relations but it is also a commodity in the marketplace. This is something that any trip to Mothercare will indicate. One might even say that fabric is a substance, the most significant substance, across whose surface the modes of Marxist commodity fetishism and psychoanalysis may and do cross.[32] And it is, by and large, through the actions of women that such an over-crossing takes place.[33]

The artist Sylvie Fleury turns shopping into an artistic action. She chooses only the most exclusive and most highly prized shops in which to gather the material for her work. She collects her purchases from such places as Chanel, Gucci, and Hermès and then lays them out in the gallery, often still in their brightly colored bags, as if she had just returned from a massive shopping spree. But her luxurious purchases are, like the sexual fetish, never actually used for the purposes for which they were designed. They and the experience of interacting with them, are obsessively preserved, never degraded by everyday use. *Wild Pair* of 1994 shows a fantastically rococo interior, empty except for an elegant *chaise longue* and perhaps fifty pairs of shoes scattered haphazardly over a Chinese rug. In the catalog of the 1995 exhibition *Fetishism: Visualising Power and Desire*, Roger Malbert describes this "careless scattering of things [as] unashamedly extravagant [and] insouciant. It hints at decadence,

Figure 3
Sylvie Fleury "Wild pair" (1994). Copyright courtesy of the artist.

the intoxication of trying on new clothes, of undressing and dressing, each time to delight in a new sensation, to be *sheathed, caressed, transfigured*."[34] But, here, as in other works, this exquisite pleasure is played out to excess.

In the 1992 video *Twinkle* a fixed camera shows a view of Fleury's feet as, again and again, she tries on a daunting variety of elaborate shoes. She appears to be engaged in an endless and frustrating attempt to find the perfect pair so that she can go out and leave the surveying camera behind. But as Malbert points out her indecision "translates into strip tease" so that it achieves no other ends than those of pleasuring the viewer and thus the perpetually staring camera becomes an act of fetishistic voyeurism.[35]

However it may appear, Fleury makes no claims to being engaged in feminist critique, rather the contrary: "I read all the women's magazines—or at least I try to. For me that's a full-time job and it inspires my work. And this is the answer to those women who think they cannot afford to do a thing like that."[36] In other words, the art gallery and the larger market system in which it plays its part allows her to indulge her consumer fetishism as a "full time job." Fleury, here, plays out the ultimate goal of every artist, as Freud had put it: fame, wealth, and the love of women, but in strategically *feminine* terms: fame, wealth, and the *love of shopping*.

Fleury's work is highly problematic in its approach to the issue of criticality. It seems on the one hand to be too heavily invested in commodity surfaces. It is too *near* to its fetishized object. Hers is a hermetically sealed cycle of gratification through acquisition and artistic representation which, in turn, stimulates *more acquisition* and sustains the constant constructive "work" of femininity as it is presented by the media. A fetishism for clothes, that Freud so easily and dismissively compares to the more theorizable perversion of his analysand, seems to be re-articulated by Fleury as an excessive self-pleasuring that effectively turns the tables on any viewer too quick to pass judgement. In the face of these images that same gallery viewer might find him/herself more than a little seduced—compromised by their fetishisms. The foibles of Western women suddenly to appear to be something singularly disconcerting. All this seems to indicate that a potential for criticality can be salvaged from within the enmeshed space of seductive surfaces because what we witness in Fleury's work is the fetish as it oscillates—*as it undoes itself*. Here the constant processes of consumer fetishism with pleasure as their ends always also suggest the impending return to a state of anxiety.

Either/Or

In his earliest discussion of the subject Freud acknowledges that "a certain degree of fetishism is habitually present in normal love, especially in those stages of it in which the normal sexual aim seems unattainable or its fulfilment prevented." Freud connects this "normal" fetishism directly to textiles in a quote from Goethe:[37]

*Get me a kerchief from her
breast,
A Garter that her knee has
pressed*[38]

Here, a certain kind of fetishism
serves to mediate between the
lover and another person.
Presumably this is the form of
fetishism to which Freud's French
contemporary, the psychiatrist
G. G. de Clérambault was thinking
of as his point of comparison
when he spoke of women's relation
to fabric as inherently selfish.
Unlike the situation in "normal
love" (and presumably, as in the
above, the orientation of such love
is from the male position) their
fetishism does not serve to
mediate between persons.
Women's love of fabric and all
its derivations is, thus, seen as
narcissistic—and implicitly
antisocial.[39]

Now, we all (men and women)
feel the caress, the insistent draw of
fabric more or less emphatically at
different moments and this
experience—this pleasure—is, as
Clérambault suggests, inherently a
"selfish" one. Freud, having
established the grounds or
"normal" fetishism, goes on to say
that:

*This situation only becomes
pathological when the longing
for the fetish passes beyond the
point of being merely a
necessary condition attached to
the sexual object and actually
takes the place of the normal
aim, and, further, when the fetish
becomes detached from a
particular individual and
becomes the sole sexual
object.*[40]

Hence, it may be said that if, in the
case of pathological fetishism, the
relationship to the body of another
person is entirely replaced by the
fetish, then, when it comes to
textiles, distinctions between the
normal and the pathological are
thoroughly confused. It may also be
possible to contend that all such
interactions with fabric tend
towards the pathological and
further that this is precisely because
our "normal" relation to fabric is
articulated in terms of
commodification. When it comes to
fabric our fetishism is *perversely
feminine*. By virtue of this perversity
we can begin to see how fetishism,
as a process of dealing with sexual
difference, disrupts all neatly
gendered categorizations.

It is interesting that, despite the
fact that psychoanalytic film theory
most often follows a Freudian/
Lacanian analytic axis, the
gendered dichotomy of male—active
and perverse versus woman—
passive and hysteric, has already
been somewhat disrupted. In his
review of "The Fetish in the Theory
and History of the Cinema" Michael
Vernet points out that Metz defines
fetishism:

*[. . .] not as a perversion but as a
psychical process characterized
by the fetishist's struggle
between belief and knowledge,
by the drive to restore a
disparaged belief (we could also
say, to repair or restore a
wounded body, since that is how
the fetishist perceives the female
body), and also by the refusal of
the fetishist to recognize sexual
difference. What is interesting
here is the hesitation, the
position of uncertainty in the*

*fetishist (whether a man or
woman): between the sexes;
between self and other—
projecting onto oneself that
which is believed to have been
seen in the other; between belief
and knowledge; and finally
between symbolic distinctions,
since the fetishist manifests a
perversion of the symbolic in so
far as it must challenge difference.*[41]
[emphasis is my own]

Now such a definition of fetishism is
useful because it transforms the
fetish from something that is
gender exclusive, the object of men
alone, into the object of a
potentially universal, and none too
private, pathology.

The challenge to difference that
fetishism stages is powerfully
articulated in the work of Cathy de
Monchaux. The early work *Erase*
(1989) is an object of half-phallic
half-labial form produced by the
bolting together of velvet, denim,
and metal joints. While it uses a
recognizably fetishistic language of
materials, the form as whole is
highly problematic as an erotic
fetish object. That is because it
singularly fails to erase the problem
of gender difference but, rather,
plays it out theatrically by flagrantly
conflating male and female genital
signifiers. Another work, *Scarring
the Wound* (1993), threads together
layers and layers of brass rib-like
(or, perhaps, phallic) forms and
folds of red velvet to produce an
elaborate arabesque that builds up
around a small heart-shaped hole. It
looks like a strange form of
ornamented trophy reminiscent of
the rosettes given to small girls at
gymkhanas. The attempt to suture
the wound is a lost cause because

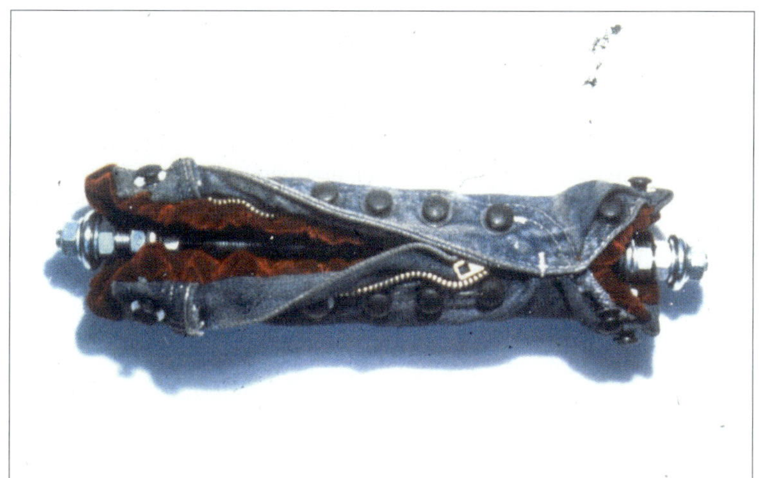

Figure 4
Cathy de Monchaux, "Erase" (1989).
Copyright courtesy of the artist.

the piling on of surfaces merely expands and enlarges the primary absence. What de Monchaux's works suggest is that fetishism touches all of us, male and female, because sex is a perpetually destabilizing force poised like a man trap to trip us up. This threat lurks in all de Monchaux's beautifully worked surfaces.

Certain of Jordan Baseman's works play out the problem of

Figure 5
Cathy de Monchaux, "Scarring the Wound" (1993). Copyright courtesy of the artist.

gender and anxieties about difference in alternative ways. *Closer to the Heart* (1994) is made up of a young boy's uniform shirt hung on a wire coat hanger. Emanating from the woven surface of one sleeve is a long fall of dark hair, each strand threaded delicately into the cloth at the shoulder. The long hair confuses gendered signifiers and transforms the crisp and neatly tailored textile object so that it appears as if it were under an attack from within. But there is no "within." The shirt is empty, marked by a reminder of an absent body. The knowledge that hair and nails continue to grow after death makes us uncannily aware of the insistence of the body and its workings which can only be temporarily tailored and contained. Like de Monchaux's works, these objects give us a sense of the gendered self in a state of extreme vulnerability.

In Basemen's work this vulnerability is linked to a specific moment in the development of the male child when he begins to be

Figure 6
Jordan Baseman, "Closer to the Heart" (1994). Copyright courtesy of the artist.

taught how to take on the masculine attributes and modes of behavior that are perceived to be socially acceptable. The hair appears like a form of hysterical symptom, the surface signs of a frantically and chaotically desiring body. The fabric is here singularly lacking in the phallic prowess seen in Alan Jones's work from the 1960s and 1970s. The threads of hair that hang from the shoulder of the shirt are more closely reminiscent of Freud's description of primitive women's supposed "shame" at their own genital deficiency. These artists' interaction with fabric work its fetishistic potential excessively and in the process tip the scales of gender and skew its accepted signs in ways that suggest a powerful critique of the social/sexual status quo.

The fetishist's disavowal, his insistence on maintaining a narcissistic belief, always has the potential to set up a scrambling in the symbolic. Fabric is able to signify "something" without that something ever being fully spoken. The fetish is silent and its secret never submits to the social/sexual order of things. It insists on playing upon us with its overt tactility. Thus fabric can be seen as a mode of experience that does not depend on the Symbolic because it is, in the most beguiling of ways, antisocial, a selfish and self-pleasuring seduction of and by the surface. Its significance is established only insofar as that symbolic order and the difference on which it depends is resisted. Such resistance is liable to repression: in the Symbolic realm we are not *supposed* to indulge in the stuff of surfaces, to be what Sacher-Masoch calls "super-

sensualists," or, at least, *not too often*. The surface is a potentially dangerous ground but the fetishist's indulgence puts paid to the idea that the *firm* structure of truth and the *malleable* surface of appearance are separate and irreconcilable entities. In doing so he/she allows for the free play of desire that is in itself a critical force to be reckoned with.

Notes

1. Christian Metz, *Psychoanalysis and Cinema: The Imaginary Signifier*, ed. Stephen Heath and Colin McCabe (London: Macmillan, 1982), p. 75.
2. Sigmund Freud (1909) quoted from "Freud and Fetishism: Previously Unpublished Minutes of the Vienna Psychoanalytic Society," ed. and trans. Louis Rose, in *Psychoanalytic Quarterly* LVII, 1988, p. 154.
3. Ibid.
4. Ibid.
5. Ibid.
6. For a comprehensive discussion of fetishism in relation to cinema and feminism see Laura Mulvey, "Some thoughts on Theories of Fetishism in the Context of Contemporary Culture," in October, no. 65, Summer 1993, pp. 3–20 and *Fetishism and Curiosity* (Bloomington, Indianapolis IN and London: Indiana University Press and the British Film Institute, 1996).
7. Mark Wigley, "Theoretical Slippage: The Architecture of Fetish," *Fetish, Princeton Architectural Journal* 14, 1992, p. 98.
8. For the history of the term fetish in its relation to colonialism see William Pietz, "The Problem of

the Fetish," *Res* 9, 1985, "The Problem of the Fetish, II, The Origins of the Fetish," *Res* 13, Spring 1987, and "The Problem of the Fetish, IIIa, Bosman's Guinea and the Enlightenment Theory," *Res* 16, 1988. There is, unfortunately, no space to develop this connection here, although this historical aspect of the fetish may also be argued as having some considerable relevance to cloth and culture.

9. David Harvey, The Condition of Postmodernity (Oxford: Basil Blackwell, 1989), p. 7, quoted by Wigley, *Fetish, Princeton Architectural Journal* 14, 1992, p. 98.

10. Wigley, in fact, attacks such a position as projecting an illusion of authority and possession and further suggests that "[t]he phallic pretension of this desire to penetrate the other organizes all the discourses that identify fetishism only in order to reject it [. . .]" as something dangerous or, rather, dangerously alluring. Wigley, ibid.

11. *The Age of Innocence* (Columbia Pictures, 1993), dr. Martin Scorsese. It is remarkable to what extent its revelations sit in opposition to the overtly phallic codes and action of the movies for which the director is better known.

12. Edith Wharton, *The Age of Innocence* (London: Penguin, 1974), p. 239.

13. It must be said that the actress, Michelle Pfeiffer, is as divinely seductive in a corset as she is in her famously fetishistic cat-suit.

14. The male child comes to believe that the idealized phallic mother has been punished by the removal of her penis and, furthermore, that he is also threatened with this fate. The female child, conversely, comes to believe that she is inadequate and can only compensate for her narcissistic wound by appropriating the *paternal* phallus. Hence, the theorizing process results in the onset of the "castration complex" in boys and "penis envy" in girls.

15. Sigmund Freud, "Fetishism" (1927), *Penguin Freud Library, Vol. 7. On Sexuality*, p. 354.

16. Ibid., pp. 354–5.

17. Edith Wharton, *The Age of Innocence* (London: Penguin, 1974), p. 90.

18. Leopold Sacher-Masoch, "Venus in Furs" in *Masochism* (New York: Zone Books, 1989), pp. 143–273.

19. Octave Mannoni, "L'Illusion comique ou le théâtre du point de vue de l'imaginaire" in *Clefs pour l'imaginaire ou l'autre scène* (Paris: Edition du Seuil, 1969), p. 180, quoted here from Christian Metz, *Psychoanalysis and Cinema: The Imaginary Signifier* (London: Macmillan, 1982), p. 71.

20. Freud and many of his followers assume that women *do not fetishize* or certainly not in the same manner. This distinction between men and women has been the grounds of heated debate in both psychoanalysis and feminist theory. See in particular Lorraine Gamman and Merja Makinen, *Female Fetishism: A New Look* (London: Lawrence & Wishart, 1994) for a comprehensive discussion of the debates in terms of cultural studies. See also Marjorie Garber, "Fetish Envy" in *October*, no. 54, Fall 1990. Emily Apter, *Feminizing the Fetish: Psychoanalysis and Narrative Obsession in Turn-of-the-Century France* (Ithaca, NY and London: Cornell University Press, 1991) and from the point of view of psychoanalysis, George Zavitzianos, "The Perversion of Fetishism in Women" in *Psychoanalytic Quarterly* LI, 1982.

21. Lacan quoted by Gamman and Makinen, *Female Fetishism: A New Look* (London: Lawrence & Wishart, 1994) p. 102. See also *Feminine Sexuality: Jacques Lacan and the École Freudienne*, eds Juliette Mitchel and Jacqueline Rose (London: Macmillan, 1982).

22. Gamman and Makinen, ibid., pp. 102–3

23. See Jacques Lacan. "The Mirror Stage as Formative of the Function of the *I* as Revealed in Psychoanalytic Experience" in *Écrits*, trans. Alan Sheriden (London and New York: Routledge, 1989), pp. 1–8.

24. Gamman and Makinen, *Female Fetishism: A New Look* (London: Lawrence & Wishart, 1994) p. 103.

25. Mary-Anne Doane, "Masquerade Reconsidered: Further Thoughts on the Female Spectator," *Discourse* 11, Fall/Winter 1988–1989, pp. 44–5, here quoted in Gamman and Makinen, ibid.

26. See George Bataille, "The Big Toe," in *Visions of Excess: Selected Writings 1927–1939*,

ed. Alan Stoekl (Minneapolis, MN: University of Minnesota Press, 1985), pp. 20–3.

27. Laura Mulvey, "Fears, Fantasies and the Male Unconscious or 'You Don't Know what is Happening, Do You, Mr. Jones?'" in *Visual and Other Pleasures* (London: Macmillan, 1989), pp. 6–13.

28. Ibid., p. 12.

29. Sigmund Freud, "Femininity" (1933) quoted in *Psychoanalysis and Gender: An Introductory Reader*, ed. Rosalind Minsky (London: Routledge, 1996), p. 232.

30. Sigmund Freud (1909) quoted from "Freud and Fetishism: Previously Unpublished Minutes of the Vienna Psychoanalytic Society," *Psychoanalysis Quarterly* LVII, 1988, pp. 155–6.

31. For the differences and similarities between the Freudian and Marxian versions of the fetish see Laura Mulvey, "Some Thoughts on Theories of Fetishism in the Context of Contemporary Culture," in *October*, no. 65, Summer 1993, pp. 3–20.

32. For Karl Marx on the "Commodity Fetish" see "The Fetishism of The Commodity and its Secret" in *Capital*, vol. 1.

33. Although it must be pointed out that many men do actually *like* to buy clothes. Would Freud have considered this "perverse?"

34. Roger Malbert, in *Fetishism: Visualising Power and Desire* (London: The South Bank Centre, 1995) p. 91.

35. Ibid., p. 92.

36. Ibid.

37. Sigmund Freud, "Three Essays on Sexuality" (1927), *Penguin Freud Library, Vol. 7, On Sexuality*, p. 66.

38. Goethe, *Faust*, Part 1, Scene 7, quoted in Sigmund Freud, ibid., p. 66.

39. See Papetti, de, Freminville *et al.* (eds) *La passion des étoffes ches un neuro-psychiatre G. G. de Clérambault* (Paris: Solin, 1981). For a discussion in English of de Clérambault and his ideas see Joan Copjec, "The Sartorial Superego," *October*, no. 50, Fall 1989, pp. 57–95.

40. Ibid., pp. 66–7.

41. Marc Vernet, "The Fetish in the Theory and History of the Cinema," in *Endless Night: Cinema and Psychoanalysis, Parallel Histories*, ed. Janet Bergstrom, (Berkeley, CA, London and Los Angeles, CA: University of California Press, 1999), p. 91.

Way Beyond Craft: Thinking through the Work of Mildred Constantine

Abstract

"Way Beyond Craft: Thinking through the Work of Mildred Constantine," examines the legacy of Mildred Constantine (American, b. 1913). As curator at the Museum of Modern Art in New York from 1948 to 1971, and co-author of *Beyond Craft: The Art Fabric* (1973) and *The Art Fabric: Mainstream* (1981), Constantine's contributions to fiber-based production throughout the 1970s and 1980s are important and have been long overlooked outside of a small constituency of artists and historians directly impacted by her work.

JENNI SORKIN

Jenni Sorkin is Research Assistant at the Museum of Contemporary Art, Los Angeles. She has written for *Art Monthly, Frieze, The New Art Examiner, NU,* and *Third Text.*

Textile, Volume 1, Issue 1, pp. 29–47
Reprints available directly from the Publishers.
Photocopying permitted by licence only.

Way Beyond Craft: Thinking through the Work of Mildred Constantine

As the progenitor of American textile exhibitions and publications, Mildred Constantine's contributions to fiber-based production throughout the 1970s and 1980s are well known and highly regarded within a small circle of museum and art departments across the United States, Canada, and Europe. Yet outside of this constituency of artists, curators, and historians directly impacted by her work, Constantine is long forgotten, her exhibitions unremembered, and the vast majority of her books and catalogs out of print.

From 1948 to 1953, Mildred Constantine (American, b. 1913) was Assistant Curator in the Department of Architecture and Design at the Museum of Modern Art in New York, and from 1953 through 1970, Associate Curator. In 1971, before her retirement, she served jointly as a consultant to the department, as well as Special Assistant to the Director of the Museum, then John B. Hightower.[1]

Constantine was one of only a handful of women in curatorial positions at the Modern,[2] working under Director Phillip Johnson, who founded the Modern's architecture program in 1932, and after 1951, his successor, Arthur Drexler.[3] During her first ten years at the museum, she assisted Johnson on a number of ambitious and important exhibitions, including *Eight Automobiles* (1950) and *Signs in the Street* (1954),[4] both of which dealt with post-war consumer culture, bringing cars and commercial signs from retailers such as Woolworth Co. into the galleries in an effort to reward good auto design and urban street signage, respectively.

Specializing in graphics, Constantine single-handedly organized exhibitions with much less fanfare and publicity, ranging from *Modern Abstract Japanese Calligraphy* (1954) to *Greetings!* (1966), a quirky exhibition of greeting cards created both by artists and industry. In her essay on Dorothy C. Miller, who was a curator at the Modern prior to, and during, Constantine's tenure, curator Lynn Zelevansky has suggested that it is "unlikely that an enterprise of great importance to the institution would have been directed by a woman . . . Having had a male director from the beginning, the Modern's most influential curators have also been men."[5]

Perhaps because of her subordinate position, Constantine has often been left out of the recent histories of the Museum of Modern Art, including the museum's own endeavor, *The Museum of Modern Art: The History and the Collection* (1984).[6] She garnered little more than a mention in Mary Anne Staniszewski's thought-provoking *The Power of Display: A History of Exhibition Installations at the Museum of*

Modern Art (1998).[7] More recently, Staniszewski writes:

Mildred Constantine made important contributions during her tenure at the Modern—but who knows what she might have achieved had there not been a glass ceiling, which blocks women from the highest reaches of power at most U.S. museums.[8]

As most women of her generation who had neither the language nor access to feminist thought, Constantine would most likely disagree with both Zelevansky's and Staniszewki's assessment of sexism at the Modern:

At MoMA, I never felt any difficulty about my being a woman. As a matter of fact, I was the only mother. My children would call on the telephone and tell Katie the operator that they

The images that appear throughout this text are works by many of the artists that appear in Constantine and Larsen's book, but were created and shown later, within the Lausanne Biennial in Lausanne, Switzerland. The author regrets that copyright clearance of the images from the books themselves were not able to be obtained in time for publication.

Figure 1
Jagoda Buic. Reflects Blancs II 1976/77.
Lausanne Biennial 8th Biennial.

*wanted to speak to Mama . . .
Alfred Barr's daughter and Rene
d'Harnoncourt's daughter, Anne,
who is in Philadelphia [currently
Director of the Philadelphia
Museum of Art], they all handed
down clothes to my daughter,
because each of them is a little
older than my daughter. Oh no,
from that point of view, if it
[sexism] existed, I was not aware
of it.[9]*

Constantine's anecdote gives the eminent Barr and d'Harnoncourt a maternal edge, presenting a kinder, gentler MoMA than history reflects today, the stuff of curatorial camaraderie and exchange, rather than masculine authority and egotism. The generational passage of children's clothing invites the metaphor of legacy, which is particularly applicable to Constantine, who is best remembered for her textile scholarship, begun while at the museum.

Avidly experimental and unusual in its scope, the Modern's design department created exhibitions that can be characterized by their commitment to modernity and mass-produced objects. Beginning with Johnson's 1934 Machine Art show, the museum focused on the best that industrial America had to offer, with wares ranging from cocktail shakers to furniture in its design galleries, while trumpeting Cubism and Surrealism in its painting and sculpture galleries. This left little room for the individual craftsperson. Although many museums acquired decorative objects into (and beyond) the twentieth century, the Modern is distinguished by its distance from arts and crafts.

Indeed, Constantine's interest in contemporary woven structures and fiber-based practice came late in her professional life, in 1962, upon meeting Sheila Hicks (American, b. 1934) in New York, through mutual friends both had in Mexico. This led her to seek out other artists who were working similarly.[10] However, it was not until 1969, after 21 years at the museum, that Constantine curated the most important show of her career at the Modern.

Reassessing weaving at mid-century, *Wall Hangings* (1969)[11] was the beginning of Constantine's subsequent involvement with textiles, as well as the initiation of a fruitful twelve-year collaboration with commercial textile designer Jack Lenor Larsen (American, b. 1927). Aware of their similar aesthetic interests and her own technological limitations, Constantine asked Larsen to serve as co-curator of the exhibition.[12] The research for the exhibition took the pair to Eastern Europe:

*I decided there was no way I
could even think about what the
field really was like unless I saw
it for myself, so with great
difficulty, I got all the visas to
Poland, Yugoslavia,
Czechoslovakia, and of course, I
was in the Soviet Union in 1969. I
was there, I met artists, I was
with the artists; it was the only
way to really find out what was
going on.[13]*

Constantine had first seen Eastern European artists through their inclusion in the 1967 Lausanne Biennial.[14] Given the restrictions places on citizens in communist countries in the late 1960s, including the freedom to travel, Constantine's visit was bold, and presumably, met with gratitude and hope. It is to her credit that she remained staunchly committed to the group of Eastern European artists selected for *Wall Hangings*; their work has continually appeared in Constantine and Larsen's successive volumes.

It is nearly impossible to determine where Constantine ends and Larsen begins; their collaboration is virtually seamless. There is a similar writing style that is consistent with her earlier museum publications, but given their brevity, it is hard to credit her as the sole author. Certainly, though, she originated *Wall Hangings*, and possibly all subsequent projects, and can be rightly viewed as the major intellectual force behind their partnership. Additionally, while Larsen published his memoirs[15] Constantine went on to write *Whole Cloth* (1997) with a different co-author, Laurel Reuter, which attests to her ongoing commitment and

Figure 2
Françoise Grossen, Daniel Graffin. Plaited Sisab plus Padded fiber 1976/77. Lausanne Biennial 8th Biennial.

interest in the field.[16] That said, it is unclear how the writing was done. When asked, Constantine responded that it was entirely collaborative, but could not elaborate regarding process.[17]

Wall Hangings

The twenty-eight artists included in *Wall Hangings* represent three distinct generations of weavers: those born in Europe at the turn of the century and educated at the Bauhaus or in traditional tapestry techniques; Europeans born before the Second World War; and Americans educated at esteemed design programs in the States in which European-trained weavers were instructors, including Black Mountain College in North Carolina, Cranbrook Academy in Michigan, the University of California at Berkeley, and the Institute of Design in Chicago. While the majority of the artists were women, three men were also included: Walter G. Nottingham (American, b. 1930), Ed Rossbach (American, b. 1914), and Herman Scholten (Dutch, b. 1932).

Artists from eight countries were represented in *Wall Hangings*, including Columbia (Olga de Amaral), Germany (Anni Albers, Gunta Stölzl), Poland (Magdalena Abakanowicz, Zofia Butrymowicz, Barbara Falkowska, Ewa Jaroszynska, Jolanta Owidzka, Wojciech Sadley), Yugoslavia (Jagoda Buic), the Netherlands (Wilhemina Fruytier, Herman Scholten), Switzerland (Marguerite

Figure 3
Jagoda Buic. Colombe 2 1986/87.
Lausanne Biennial 1987, 13th Biennial.

Carau, Elsi Giauque, Françoise Grossen, Annemarie Klinger, Moik Schiele), Canada (Mariette Rousseau-Vermette), and the United States (Evelyn Anselevicius, Thelma Becherer, Sheila Hicks, Walter G. Nottingham, Ed Rossbach, Kay Sekimachi, Sherri Smith, Lenore Tawney, Susan Weitzman).

Wall Hangings (1969) had all the trappings of a modern international style, with woven structures that emphasized formal, academic attributes such as symmetry and color over technique and materials. This was accomplished through the visual finesse of the catalog: large black-and-white photographs of each artwork were paired with the requisite listing of materials, but omitted an explanation as to how the piece was created. To emphasize technique in a craft-dominant medium would be to diminish its complexity as an art object. While MoMA had held *Textiles U.S.A.*, an exhibition of industrial textiles, a decade earlier,[18] this was the first time the museum had sponsored a group show of individual artists, both men and women, working in fiber. Most crucial was the exhibition's location on the first floor of the museum, rather than its segregation in the design department, located on the third floor.[19] Medium hierarchy is still an issue at many traditional and encyclopedic museums, with the "low" or "minor" arts such as ceramics, textiles, and photography literally shown at a level below the floors devoted to European painting, drawing, and sculpture.

The work featured in *Wall Hangings* was varied and vast: the hard, bright geometry of Albers' and Stölzls's earliest Bauhaus contributions to the bunched, tight masses of cotton rope in Fruytier's heavy, undulating tapestries; from Butrymowicz's dark hairy sunrise to Sekimachi's airy, monofilament mobile floating from the ceiling. Such work was closer in look and feel to the bright washes and violent strokes of abstract expressionist painting than the pictorial tapestry favored in European craft guilds.

Constantine and Larsen's brief catalog essay grapples with a context for the artworks' origins, beginning at the beginning of time:

In the early phases of almost every culture, basketry, fish traps, and even shelters often shared a common technology with fabric.[20]

This is what I will term the "creation approach," reaching back into the muddle of prehistory to reference the necessity of knotting, braiding, and netting to such tasks as building, dwelling, and feeding. Such a strategy assumes the timelessness and naturalism of fiber while introducing the concept of technology, which quickly paves the way to industrial production and notions of "progress." As though dumbfounded by the beauty and originality of their discovery, the authors dole out terms: Bauhaus weavers are paired with "machine aesthetic," while weaving by Polish nationals is explained as "an art of the people."[21] The authors continually vacillate between the ancient and the modern, recalling "Pre-Columbian weaving" and "synthetic materials" in the same breath, defying time and space in homage to the work itself.[22] There is a strong sense of process, a kind of thinking out loud, with Constantine and Larsen struggling to define a medium that had unhinged itself from the toil, labor, and necessity of what weaving and tapestry once were, and instead, allied itself with the aesthetics and principles of modernism. The resulting work was a spirited and far-reaching experiment in materials, shape, and form. With much of the work unhindered by a loom, the authors emphasize the freedom and flexibility of the materials, as if the weavings could adapt to any medium. This was a particular strength and dearly held belief on the part of Constantine, who maintains that she continually sought to defy the categories of "fine art" and "craft."[23]

Undoubtedly, *Wall Hangings* set Constantine on a new path. Upon retiring from the Modern, two years later, in 1971, she flourished, rather than faded. Although she was not an active or even self-described participant, Constantine's retirement coincides with the rise of the feminist movement. At age 58, her decision to continue to work without institutional affiliation parallels the experiences of many women who were achieving independence for the first time. Extremely prolific in the decade after her retirement, it is my belief that Constantine did her most important work upon leaving the Museum of Modern Art.

Beyond Craft

In collaboration with Larsen, *Beyond Craft: The Art Fabric* was published in 1973.[24] Nearly three-hundred pages, the oversized volume offers a colorful history of the 1960s through the work of twenty-eight artists, all but two of whom had previously appeared in *Wall Hangings*.[25] In keeping with books of its time, each artist entry is accompanied by an attractive black-and-white photograph of the artist at work, along with a text describing their practice. Highly gendered, the men are sullen and serious, while the women smile or pose for the camera. Bibliography is the reigning methodology, painstakingly tracing each artist's educational background, influences, travels, and artistic lineage. There is a journalistic style to the writing, brisk reportage combined with an extreme editorial slant that comments inappropriately on nationality ("Aurelia Muñoz is deeply and intensely Spanish . . .");[26] personality ("Dick Landis is a loner . . . Direct and independent, neither shy nor impressionable, he is aloof from city ways, unflinching and unaffiliated")[27] and beauty ("Wilhelmina Fruytier, a tall handsome woman, is well cast.")[28] Strangely suggestive, the collaborative couple Ritzi and Peter Jacobi are declared a "swinging couple" at the beginning of their entry, and later confirmed as "free of inhibition." An odd turn of phrase, it is easily misconstrued.[29]

Collectively, the artists are awarded the distinction of "genius,"[30] and individual artworks are routinely described as "visionary" or "timeless." However, a hierarchy exists, where Magdalena Abakanowicz (Polish, b. 1932) and Sheila Hicks are the

Figure 4
Ritzi Jacobi. La Derniere de Cette Series 1986/87. Lausanne Biennial 1987, 13th Biennial.

most celebrated artists of the book, each given between six and eight pages of full-color reproductions and longer, more analytical texts.

Commencing with the title of the volume, Constantine and Larsen clearly define their usage of "art fabric," devising several criteria for their creation: construction (woven on- or off-loom); a work's relationship to tradition (situating it within a lineage of both tapestry and the avant-garde); and authorship (ingenuity, genius, and progress for the field at large). An art fabric itself falls into one of three clearly delineated categories:

1. A wall hanging (illustrated in the previous volume, but expanded upon here),
2. An environment, or
3. An assemblage.

Figure 5
Jagoda Buic. Reflects Blancs II 1976/77. Lausanne Biennial 8th Biennial.

Well versed in both craft history and modernism, Constantine authors an introductory history that joins her two concerns. Intertwining the art nouveau movement in Britain with the formation of the Bauhaus, she traces a lineage of ideas that traverse the Atlantic along with the exiled artists, and are spread through their subsequent tenures in the U.S. as esteemed and influential master craftspeople at Black Mountain College, University of California at Berkeley, California College of Arts and Crafts, and Cranbrook Academy.

Within this known history exists an unfamiliar one. Constantine provides a chronological narrative of exhibitions that have concentrated exclusively on textiles, including the origins of the Lausanne Biennial and the Milan Triennial. As a curator, she was keenly aware of the activities of other curators, and their exhibitions. *Beyond Craft* includes dates, venues, curatorial information, and partial lists of artists for pioneering exhibitions that have all but vanished, including: *Perspectief in Textiel* (Stedelijk Museum, Amsterdam, 1969), *Experiencas Artisticas Textiles* (Museo de Arte Contemporáneo, Madrid), her own *Wall Hangings* (Museum of Modern Art, New York, 1969), and *Deliberate Entanglements* (University of California at Los Angeles, 1971).

Figure 6
Urszula Plewka-Schmidt. Symbols 1978.
1979 9th Biennial, Lausanne Biennial.

With the history of contemporary exhibitions and exhibition practice still a recent art historical phenomenon, museums' exhibition archives from thirty years ago are not nearly as meticulous, complete, or even accessible as they are now. In most cases, they do not exist past a few slides, photographs, a press release, and an out-of-print catalog.

Factor in poor storage conditions, careless handling, and multiple building relocations, and they are just as likely to be lost or destroyed. Additionally, within the current climate of budget cuts and staff shortages, the museum's archives are often among the areas to lose funding because they service only scholars and a few others.

Files on artists, curators' notes and correspondence can be useful and telling mementos, enlightening the process and thinking behind an exhibition. Additionally, written exhibition records can complicate individual artist histories, offering everything from new ideas about the context surrounding the work's production to hard-to-find

Figure 7
Wojech Sadley, Gilles Morrisette, Helen McGregor. Works from Association. Pierre Pauli installed Salts Mill, Bradford, 1990.

provenance history. In lieu of such documents, installation photographs, recording the exhibition's hang, can offer an invaluable visual record of an exhibition that is obscure, known by name only, or is altogether forgotten, both at an individual and institutional level. Constantine's inclusion of installation photographs for textile exhibitions of the late 1960s is arguably the most important feature of *Beyond Craft*. While a visual record can never provide a complete and accurate picture of an exhibition, it still provides useful insight into a past event. What a show looked

Figure 8
Gerhardt Knodel: Entracte. Lausanne Biennial 1983, 11th Biennial.

like, and the manner in which it was hung (whether by chronology, nationality, medium, or theme), can challenge the ways in which we see or assume the past. Were works grouped according to medium or style? Was nationality or region a consideration? Are works hung from the ceiling? Do they have ample space? Is anything hung in an interesting or out-of-the-ordinary way, such as blocking a doorway or touching the ground? Or is the hang rather conservative and uneventful? Finally, seeing a photograph of a room full of fiber works offers a greater context for an individual artwork, both then and now.

With her keen curatorial eye, Constantine addresses some of these crucial details:

Installation photographs only partially reveal the enormous success of a sensitive mounting by curator Wil Bertheux. Of all the major group shows during the last several years, "Perspectief in Textiel" was without peer. Part of its success derived from the generous space allowed—only two to each gallery—so that the works could be viewed independently. The respectful omission of all props and diversions and the soft, even

flood of natural overhead light were also contributing factors . . . This photograph shows the affinity between the pendulous work of Sadley and the shaped weaving of Vohanka.[31]

In a medium of highly detailed work, slides and photographs are required to reflect the size and experience of an individual piece, rather than an overall feeling of the space it inhabits, as well as the space it shares with other works. To see installation photographs is to make connections between seemingly disparate works, and to reflect on ways in which artists are

Figure 9
Magdalena Abakanowicz. Abakan Red, 1970–73. Installed Lausanne Biennial 1995. Parallel Histories 16th Biennial of Lausanne.

influenced and in dialogue with each other. Moreover, the international shows were events on the cutting edge, showing now-iconic works for the first time, and introducing artists from around the globe to work that was new, unknown, or in the case of the Eastern-bloc countries, inaccessible.

In *Beyond Craft*, the installation photographs appear beyond group exhibitions, and also occur within individual artist entries, documenting solo shows at now-defunct galleries in both the U.S. and Europe.

There is a frustrating, albeit entirely modernist, universalism

Figure 10
Olga de Amaral Paysage Calicanto 1981. Association: Pierre Pauli (from Bradford Salts Mill, 1990).

Figure 11
Urszula Plewka-Schmidt. Madonna 1983. 11th Biennial Lausanne, Biennial.

present in *Beyond Craft*. Inherently apolitical, the authors fail to contextualize the political, social, and economic circumstances of artists working in different regions of Europe and the U.S. The artistic lineages created between the Bauhaus and U.S. institutions are far more complex than suggested; artists of the same generation likely had more in common, aesthetically and politically, than sixty-something refugees and their twenty-something Master of Fine Arts (MFA) students. Neither do they address the differences between the educational structures in Eastern Europe, versus the idealist American utopias (such as Black Mountain and Cranbrook) that emerged post-war. What did freedom—aesthetic, intellectual, artistic, political—mean in different locales, and what consequences did it have? Such extreme and obvious differences necessitate the presence of a socio-political context.

Neatly organized by artist, *Beyond Craft* was an exhibition catalog for an exhibition that did not occur, providing a roster of artists and a selection of works that are reproduced throughout the text, accompanied by brief artist entries. Using a simple and straightforward format, the book highlights the contributions of twenty-eight artists from eight countries, broadening the scope of fiber-based production beyond the borders of the U.S.

Constantine and Larsen's follow-up volume, *The Art Fabric: Mainstream* (1981), came almost a decade later.[32] If *Beyond* Craft was an unactualized exhibition, then *Mainstream* went the extra step as a book that strove to maintain its independence from the brief life span of a show. Constantine and Larsen's follow-up book is broader in scope than its sister text, organized into sections on materials, histories and techniques, rather than by artist. The authors cover exhibitions of the 1970s, as well as the expansion of the medium into new areas of architecture, landscape, and theatrical design. An exhibition by the same name was circulated by the American Federation of the Arts, and was shown at the San Francisco Museum of Modern Art the same year. Because the book does not contain a checklist, it is impossible to know either which artists and works were included in the show without access to the exhibition files.

Ostensibly tailored to an audience beyond the art world, *Mainstream* begins with a historical framework identical to the previous volume, providing a summary of concepts introduced earlier, as well as initiating an interesting and important discussion on the large scale of works produced throughout the 1960s, influenced by the oversized canvases elemental to abstract expressionism.[33] The title itself, *The Art Fabric: Mainstream*, is a continuation of the second half of *Beyond Craft*. It is a curious selection worth reconsideration; to venerate something as "mainstream" is to acknowledge its previous obscurity. In 1989, a show by the title of *Making Their Mark: Women Artists Move Into the Mainstream, 1970–1982*[34] circulated throughout the U.S. Highlighting the contributions of feminist artists of the 1970s, the checklist was filled with numerous under-known artists, mixed with a handful of well-represented painters and sculptors. Artists working in that decade may have had a few years in the spotlight, but overall, there was very little mainstream to speak of, resulting in a generation of artists with neither gallery representation nor tenure.

Constantine and Larsen's version of the "mainstream" proves to be similar. Was the Art Fabric at its height of recognition in the early years of the 1980s? The year 1981 is simultaneously close and far enough from the 1970s to capture it both textually and visually. The authors devise a survey book that is thematic rather than chronological, single-handedly authoring the aesthetics of the period through detailed discussions on materials and techniques, highlighting the widespread interest in found fabrics and unspun fibers. Raw and hairy, "shaggy" is best remembered as a dominant style, museum wall thick with fringed hangings in rusty oranges and olive greens, while macramé was all the rage on the domestic front.

The third and final volume of the Constantine/Larsen trilogy,[35] *Mainstream*'s selection of artists is easily anticipated, with those previous making appearances through a selection of new and older works. However, a much larger variety of artists are represented visually, illustrating a term or technique through careful descriptions of individual works. More than sixty artists appear throughout the book, a number of them emerging.

Geared toward a museum audience, *Mainstream* has a tendency toward the didactic, with a large glossary, an index, and an artists' biography section. It also works to keep up with the latest trends, including a section on corporate commissions, the slick 1980s concoction of art and business. This is a far cry from the smiling photo of Sheila Hicks with her backstrap loom, weaving alongside the indigenous women of Mexico.[36] Large color photos abound of hotels and embassy lobbies filled with structures of fabric paralyzed mid-air, fashioned into abstracted kites or birds.

Regardless of the quality of such work, Constantine and Larsen's scholarship is unique in its wholly visual orientation, offering a dazzling array of installation photos that go beyond the boundaries of the museum and into other privatized spheres, such as the theater or the office building. The presence of a new market for large-scale, permanent installations is twofold: insuring sponsorship and interest outside of the museum, and in accordance the long-held design principle of utilitarianism, proving the massive and heavy con-structions indeed had highly valued applications as a buffer of sound, or as a component of interior design.

As in *Beyond Craft*'s introduction, *Mainstream*'s chapter-long focus on exhibitions of the 1970s proves to be the most pertinent and important contribution the book makes toward the preservation of textile history. Offering spots of highly detailed information, the authors provide background, where they can, of the curator's intentions and interests. They also include a large assortment of installation photographs from exhibitions large and small, from the 1977 Lausanne Biennial, to a group show of young Bay Area artists in 1979 at Louise Aldrich Gallery in San Francisco.

Exhibitions are, by their very nature, ephemeral events, less permanent than the artworks they house and promote. Far ahead of its time, Constantine's continuous inclusion of exhibition and installation photographs offers a selective visual history of textile exhibitions during the primary two decades of the fiber arts movement. That there were far more textile-based exhibitions in the 1960s and 1970s than there are now, both on a local and international scale, goes almost without saying. As the only historian of the period, Constantine and Larsen's books remain crucial as historical documents of the field, concerned with the legacy of artists of the time period, as well as long-forgotten exhibition history.

It is interesting that in Constantine's quest to merge craft and fine-art history, she leaves out a number of very established individual artists such as Christo, Janis Kounellis, Eva Hesse, and Robert Morris, who were working with fiber materials throughout the 1960s and 1970s. Less associated with materials than movements, such artists were, with the exception of Kounellis, New York-based, and not a part of the international Art Fabric circuit, comprised of the European Biennials and Triennials. These shows carried the fatal branding of "tapestry" or "craft," and moreover, were survey shows organized around a single material rather than thematically or conceptually.

Wholly a product of the Modern, Constantine spent her formative years during the most creative and exciting era of the museum's history, a time of immense experimentation. Constantine transferred such principles to her work within *Beyond Craft: The Art Fabric* and *The Art Fabric: Mainstream*, pursuing a history in a field that lacked coherence and unification, divided by geography and without necessary and sustained critical attention within the U.S. The sheer magnitude of Constantine and Larsen's books demand, and achieve, the stature of singularity. Likewise, Constantine remains the only American historian and critic to focus on fiber-based production. Her books are profound achievements in the field. They should be in print for future generations of scholars and students.

Acknowledgments

The author wishes to thank Mary Anne Staniszewski for her time and commitment to the MoMA material and Mary Jane Jacob for generously providing a copy of her essay on Constantine, "Beyond Craft: Curating for Change," from the catalog *Small Works in Fiber, The Mildred Constantine Collection* (Cleveland OH: The Cleveland Museum of Art, 1993), now out of print.

Notes

1. The position of museum director was turbulent in the years after Rene d'Harnoncourt's retirement in 1968, and before Richard Oldenburg arrived in 1972. Bates Lowry was museum director from 1968–1969, and John B. Hightower from 1970–1972. The year of Constantine's departure in 1971 saw one of the worst Professional and Administrative Staff Association (PASTA) strikes in museum history.
2. Others included Dorothy C. Miller and Greta Daniel. While Miller was a curator in the Department of Painting and Sculpture, she was primarily founding director Alfred Barr's assistant and right hand from

1934 until his dismissal in 1943. In 1947, she was named Curator of Museum Collections, a position she occupied until 1967. Greta Daniel was Associate Curator in the Department of Industrial Design (see Note 3) throughout the 1940s and into the early 1950s, until ill health forced her to leave. Constantine succeeded Daniel as Associate Curator in the Department of Architecture and Design in 1953.

3. Phillip Johnson's history is complicated; he left the museum in 1935 under Barr and returned under d'Harnoncourt in 1949 after acquiring a degree in architecture from Harvard. The Architecture and Design department, previously split into Architecture and Industrial Design, was reunified under his directorship in 1949. Johnson left the museum for good just six years later, in 1954, to pursue architecture full time. Arthur Drexler joined the department in 1951, took over Johnson's administrative duties, and in 1956, was named Director of the Department of Architecture and Design.

4. For an in-depth discussion of both shows, see Mary Anne Staniszewski's *The Power of Display: A History of Exhibition Installations at the Museum of Modern Art* (Boston MA: MIT Press, 1998), pp. 190–4.

5. Lynn Zelavansky, "Dorothy Miller's 'Americans,' 1942–1963," *Studies in Modern Art*, no. 4 (New York: The Museum of Modern Art, 1994), p. 68. Currently Chief Curator at the Los Angeles County Museum of Art, Zelavansky worked as Curator at the Modern in the Department of Painting and Sculpture in the early 1990s.

6. Sam Hunter, *The Museum of Modern Art: The History and the Collection* (New York: Abrams, 1984). The second edition was printed in 1991. Constantine does not even appear in the index of Hunter's volume, and no mention is made throughout his extended introduction or in the subsequent short essay on the Department of Architecture and Design.

7. Mary Anne Staniszewski, ibid., pp. 192–3. Constantine is mentioned as a collaborator on the Signs in the Street show, and is credited as co-curator in the captions that appear alongside the reproduced installation shots of the exhibition.

8. Mary Anne Staniszewski, e-mail to the author, 9 August 2002.

9. Mildred Constantine, interview with the author, 5 June 2002.

10. Ibid.

11. *Wall Hangings* was on view from 25 February to 4 May 1969.

12. Mildred Constantine, interview with the author, 5 June 2002.

13. Ibid.

14. The Bienniale Internationale de la Tapisserie was initiated in Lausanne, Switzerland in 1962, and ran through 1996.

15. Larsen, Jack Lenor. *Jack Lenor Larsen: A Weaver's Memoir* (New York: Abrams, 1998).

16. Constantine, Mildred and Laurel Reuter. *Whole Cloth*. (New York: The Monacelli Press, 1997).

17. Mildred Constantine, interview with the author, 5 June 2002.

18. *Textiles U.S.A.* (1956) was part of the Good Design series held at MoMA, in collaboration with The Merchandise Mart in Chicago.

While a few artists, such as Lenore Tawney and Lyn Alexander, were included, the show emphasized commercial textile design and domestic furnishings.

19. Constantine maintains that she fought for the first floor.

20. Mildred Constantine and Jack Lenor Larsen. "Introduction," *Wall Hangings* (New York: Museum of Modern Art, 1969), unpaginated.

21. Ibid.

22. Ibid.

23. Mildred Constantine, interview with the author, 5 June 2002.

24. Mildred Constantine and Jack Lenor Larsen. *Beyond Craft: The Art Fabric* (New York: Van Nostrand Reinhold, 1973).

25. Aurelia Muñoz (Spanish, b. 1926) and Richard Landis (American, b. 1931) were not in *Wall Hangings*.

26. *Beyond Craft*, p. 208.

27. Ibid., p. 205.

28. Ibid., p. 153.

29. While this kind of commentary unfortunately still persists, with the advent of feminist and post-colonial scholarship, such language no longer goes unchecked.

30. *Beyond Craft*, p. 7.

31. Ibid., p. 57.

32. Mildred Constantine and Jack Lenor Larsen. *The Art Fabric: Mainstream* (New York and Tokyo: Kodansha International Ltd., 1981).

33. Ibid., p. 20.

34. *Making Their Mark: Women Artists Move Into the Mainstream*, ed. Randy Rosen (New York: Abbeville Press, 1989).

35. *Wall Hangings* (1969), *Beyond Craft: The Art Fabric* (1973), *The Art Fabric: Mainstream* (1981).

36. *Beyond Craft*, p. 172.

Maculate Conceptions

Abstract

This article considers the signification of and affective response to spots, dots, blotches, and patches in a number of different areas of social and cultural history in Western Europe. It attempts to account for why it is so odd or difficult to clothe or surround oneself with patterns of spots in clothing, fabric and furnishings, approaching this analysis through reflections on the idiom and appearance of the spotted in nature, religion, cosmetics, and design. The article has four sections. The first considers the history of stigmatization through the "yellow badge" that Jews and other groups have been required to wear in Europe from medieval to modern times. The second considers the meanings of patched, pied or motley clothing, especially as worn by fools. The third investigates the practice of "patching," or applying beauty spots to the face, and reactions to it during the seventeenth century. The final section considers the remarkable change of value of the spotted or mottled from the twentieth century onwards; from arousing suspicion, disgust and hostility, spotted designs evoke the richness and diversity of the world conceived, in William James's terms, as a pluralistic mosaic, clinging together by its edges.

STEVEN CONNOR

Steven Connor is Professor of Modern Literature and Theory at Birkbeck College, London. He is the author of books on Dickens, Beckett, Joyce, and post-war British fiction, as well as of *Postmodernist Culture* (1989, 2nd edn 1996), *Theory and Cultural Value* (1992) and *Dumbstruck: A Cultural History of Ventriloquism* (2000). His book *Skin: An Historical Poetics* will be published by Reaktion Books in 2003. Much of his work, including unpublished papers and work in progress, is to be found on his website at www.bbk.ac.uk/eh/skc

Textile, Volume 1, Issue 1, pp. 49–63
Reprints available directly from the Publishers.
Photocopying permitted by licence only.
© 2003 Berg. Printed in the United Kingdom.

Maculate Conceptions

Yet here's a spot. (Macbeth v.i. 30)

What do spots mean? I want in what follows to consider the signification of and affective response to different kinds of spots, dots, blotches, and patches in a number of different areas of social and cultural history in Western Europe. I will try to account for why it is so odd or difficult to clothe or surround oneself with patterns of spots in clothing, fabric, and furnishings, approaching this analysis through reflections on the idiom and appearance of the spotted in nature, religion, story, and technology.

The ways of seeing, feeling, and reading that I convene here are given encouragement and example by Michel Pastoureau's investigations of motifs of color and design, especially in his remarkable meditation on the cultural history of stripes. In *The Devil's Cloth*, Pastoureau has traced the evolution of the stripe in clothing, flags, and other fabrics and related it to attitudes towards the stripe in nature. Just as striped animals are thought of as cruel, unnatural, and even deformed, the stripe when worn becomes the mark of the outcast, or the aberration. Medieval prostitutes were often striped, as were lepers, jugglers, and clowns. Medieval devils were also often kitted out in what might seem to us now to be incongruously jazzy stripes. The bar sinister in heraldry signifies the disfigurement of illegitimacy (while also legitimating it). As a semiotic setting-apart of that which must be excluded from orderly social life, stripes exercise a disciplinary force too, as is borne out by their use for military uniform and prison clothing. With the unrelenting on–off, black–white binarism of its parallel lines, the stripe is almost a visible allegory of those forms of barely licit existence that live parallel to, but apart from, normal social life.[1]

For the greater part of human history, during which the understanding of the interior processes of the body has been extremely limited, disease has been understood in terms of its manifestations on the outside of the body. More than any other sign, it has been spots that have signified the onset of disease, whether smallpox, bubonic plague (named after its characteristic "bubos"), or any one of the host of scarcely differentiated "spotted fevers." Spots rarely if ever suggest health or vitality. The two apple-red blotches that give a healthy or lubricious glow to cheeks in Donald McGill cartoons are hugely outnumbered by more ominous rubrications and floreations on the skin—the ruddiness of the imminent apoplectic, the consumptive's hectic flush. Irregularly spotted fabrics are ominous not just because they are reminiscent of blemishes on the skin, but also because they are uncomfortable reminders of the ominous markings of other fabrics: the blood in the handkerchief that was a traditional sign of tuberculosis, and the "spotting," as it is still commonly called, which may presage a miscarriage in early pregnancy. Desdemona's strawberry-spotted handkerchief, which leads to such disaster in *Othello*, joins together the associations of disease, deception, lust and corruption.

Perhaps the two diseases most commonly associated with the appearance of spots in the medieval world were leprosy and syphilis. Spots became the identifying characteristic in emblematic representations of lepers in the medieval period, even though spots are not necessarily characteristic of the disease after its onset.[2] Medieval representations of biblical victims of skin disease such as Job and Namaan (II Kings 5) show them covered in spots, and the heroine in Robert Henryson's *Testament of Cresseid* (c. 1470) who is "with fleshelie lust sa maculait" after leaving her lover Troilus is blasted with a plague of "spottis blak" which seems to be leprosy.[3] The closeness of the link is indicated by the fact that the common name for measles seems to derive from the Middle English adjective *mesel*, or *mesyl*, meaning leprous. *Mesel* is actually a shortening of the Latin *misellus*, the diminutive of *miser*, wretched; when the word measles generated its own adjective in the nineteenth century, it shifted its emphasis, for "measly" now does not mean full of misery, but rather contemptibly poor.

However, close attention to the detailed instructions and precautions prescribed in Leviticus 13 reveals a striking fact about what the spotted seems to have meant in ancient Judaism. For it is not the extent of disease that seems to decide the degree of uncleanness, but rather the mingling of the pure and the impure. The priest presented with a man who has "in the skin of his flesh a rising, or a scab, or a bright spot" must pronounce him unclean, especially when "the appearance of the plague be deeper than the skin of his flesh" (Lev. 13.2, 3). The spreading or breaking out of spots over the skin is also a sign of leprosy, but only if the spread is not total. Remarkably, in this case, "if the leprosy break out abroad in the skin and the leprosy cover all the skin of him that hath the plague from his head even to his feet . . . he shall pronounce him clean that hath the plague: it is all turned white: he is clean" (Lev. 13.12, 13). So, for Old Testament Judaism, it is the degree of motley or mingling that determines uncleanness, not the extent of the disease. To be totally unclean is to be clean. It is for this reason that the book of Leviticus pays such close attention also to the determination of uncleanness in fabrics (Lev. 13, 47–59) and even in the walls of dwellings (Lev. 14, 33–57). The presence of a greenish or reddish plague "whether it be in warp, or woof; of linen, or of woollen, whether in a skin, or in anything made of skin" (Lev. 14, 48–9) signifies a leprous despoiling of the integrity of the fabric and is therefore unclean. When it comes to the uncleanness of leprosy (which seems to mean, tautologically, the uncleanness of mixture rather than the disease now called by the name of leprosy), there is no distinction to be made between different kinds of skin. So fabrics can suffer from the malady of spotting, as well as figure it; they can embody the uncleanness of the sign as well as be the sign of the unclean. This feeling will linger long into the later history of fabric and pattern.

Stigma

Spots are like stripes in making evident and emphatic the difference between what is socially approved or included and what is disapproved and outlawed. But the fact that the area of intersection of spots and stripes is so extensive can also disclose some striking differences between them. The point of the stripe is to mark an absolute and unconditional boundary between the included and the excluded. Those marked off with the stripe are outlandish, visibly set apart. The stripe images and effects a permanent and absolute altering of their condition. But the horror and dread of the spot is that it invades, supervening upon and coexisting with a previously clear and unspotted countenance. Indeed, one might say, in accord with the Levitican principle of uncleanness, that, where only the corrupt can be striped, *only the pure can be spotted*. It is almost better to be wholly given over to sin or crime than to bear the foul taint of partial corruption. The striped one is a renegade: the spotted one is an apostate. This, perhaps, is why knights like Clitophon in Sidney's *Arcadia* live under the motto of the ermine: "Rather dead than spotted."[4]

Much of the symbolism of stripes may rest on the fact that regular stripes are relatively rare in nature. For this reason, stripes will usually suggest some purposeful marking out or setting apart. Through signifying some design, stripes suggest the hand of some artificer, or even an act of self-designation. Spots, on the other hand, are not at all rare in nature (nor, in fact, are streaks and striations, which may approximate to stripes but are importantly distinct from them). So where the stripe is the uniform of the regulated irregular, spots are the oyxmoronic sign of the involuntary, the random, the impermanent, the formless. Stripes are formed and exhibited, but spots seem simply to happen. In performing its work of marking off, the stripe always also exhibits itself *as* a marking off, designating its own act of designation, which explains its prominence in forms of identification, flags, banners, and uniforms. But the spot is often characterized by a certain ambivalence as to whether it is a determinate mark or not. The stripe marks off a boundary within the language of signs; spots inhabit a more dubious boundary between the signifying and the nonsignifying.

The history of stigmatization in the West has a close and formative relation to the experience of spots. In Europe this has come to be associated in particular with the enforced stigmatization of Jews. The compulsory wearing of the yellow star that was "revived" in Nazi Germany had not in fact been uniformly applied in medieval Europe, and more common than the star in a number of countries was a spot or roundel, which could be red or white as well as yellow (it was known in Germany as "*der gelber Fleck*," the yellow smirch). The increasing discredit of yellow in Europe from the late medieval period onwards probably determined the settling on this color, but what seemed to matter most was that Jews should wear a color that clearly contrasted with the predominating color of their costume.[5] England was the first country in Europe to implement the recommendations of the Fourth Lateran Council of 1215 that Jews wear a distinctive mark, but Henry III's decree of 1217 called for Jews to wear two bands of white linen, inscribed with the Ten Commandments. Five years later the Council of Oxford changed this requirement, insisting instead that the color of the badge be different from the color of the garment to which it is affixed, perhaps in response to attempts by Jews to camouflage their badges by wearing white.[6] Jews, it seems, must be marked off in the very motley, or doubling of fabric which Leviticus proscribes (Lev. 19.19), such that even the cleanness of white (the ironic color of leprosy) could render them unclean. The doubleness regarding the badge of Judaism may derive partly from the Levitican vigilance against the spotting of the skin, which seems to prescribe a heightened, phobic attention to the condition of the skin of the Jews. Jews are made to wear stigmata on their skin as a turning back on them of their own cultural horror at the disfigured or unclean skin. Their enforced maculation makes them stand for the very principle of uncleanness their own religious regulations did so much to establish in Christian Europe.

However, it is a striking fact that such prescription of colors and forms is a feature both of persecuting authorities and of Jewish self-regulation, sometimes acting in close cooperation. The logic of stigma is always that of a mark given to the skin from the outside which is meant to witness or double the skin's own spontaneous auto-inscription. There are times when it seems equally desirable for both persecutor and persecuted, though for opposite reasons, that mingling or assimilation be resisted. One might recall here the fact that the mark of Cain was given by God to the first murderer, not in order to disgrace him, but in order to mark him out as God's and protect him from assault (*Genesis* 4.15). The strange interplay between a mark that wounds and a mark that affords protection, which is also enacted through Hawthorne's *The Scarlet Letter*, has been seen again recently. When the Taliban issued a fatwa in May 2001 ordering members of the tiny Hindu minority in Afghanistan to wear a badge of yellow, the justification, actually apparently accepted by at least one Hindu religious leader, was that it would protect Hindus from punishment for infraction of Muslim law.[7]

Motley

One way to make the spotted secure is to geometrize the spots, make spots approximate to line and grid. Another way is to create a category of the spotted. The stripe sets apart the harlot, the heretic, the convict. Since the late medieval period, it has been conventional for the figure of the fool to be thought of as dressed in motley, that apotheosis of the spotted, in which miscellaneity has overwhelmed the ground on which it has arisen, forming a surface made up of shreds and patches, cross-woven, colors flung together as chance and circumstance dictate.[8] The wearing of motley allows the figure of the fool to inhabit the borderline between nature and culture (fools are "naturals"), intention and accident (is the fool ingenious or ingenuous, deliberately witless, or accidentally wise?). The word "patch" has also been applied since the late sixteenth century to a clown, fool or dolt, though "patching" came to mean not only a harmless kind of fooling, but also a more deceitful or treacherous kind of trickery. "Patch" was the nickname given to Sexton, Cardinal Wolsey's jester, and the players in Shakespeare's *Midsummer Night's Dream* are called "a crew of patches" (iii.ii. 9), a fact of which Bottom reminds us and himself when, after waking, and trying to recall his transformation, he decides that "man is but a patch'd foole, if he will offer to say, what me-thought I had" (*MND*, iv.i. 215). This usage has probably dictated the passage of the name across to the innumerable, cutely mischievous pets who have been called "Patch" and "Spot."

However, motley has a more complex history than the familiar image of the parti-colored jester or the checkered harlequin might suggest. Leslie Hotson suggests in his *Shakespeare's Motley* that Shakespeare and his contemporaries mean something very different from these gaudy pied colors when they use the word "motley." He argues that this term names, not a checkered design, but rather a form of cloth, made of closely interwoven threads, and thus exhibiting a rather coarse or even drab appearance. It is for this reason, he argues, that such motley was often named after its predominating shade, usually brown, green or yellow, a fact that is hard to reconcile with the idea of clearly distinguished and competing colors.[9] Insisting that "*motley* was not at all a gaudy parti-color, but an undemonstrative vesture of humility,"[10] Hotson aims to mark a gap between the crude antics of traditional clowns and fools and sadder, subtler, less obtrusive kinds of fool, typified by actors like Robert Arnim, for whom Shakespeare began to write in the later 1590s.

In fact, however, there may be a closer equivalence than Hotson allows between what can be called mixed motley and pied motley. In both cases, the distinction between figure and ground that allows the spot to stand out against a continuous surface has given way. In the case of mixed motley, the principle of particulation has, as it were, sunk deep into the fabric. In the case of the more traditional kind of pied motley, which seems to be a formalization of a costume made up entirely of patches, the principle of particulation has been taken up into a fabric that is all surface. In such a fabric, the abutting of edge against edge does the duty done by the superimposition of pattern upon ground and in which the "against" has therefore taken the place of the "upon." But in both mixed and pied motley, particulation is all there is.

The suspicion of patched or pied colors in medieval Europe was probably because they suggested this abundance of seams or edges. The avoidance of the seam even extended to the dividing of clothes, either at the waist or the crotch, neither of which became common in

Europe until after the fifteenth century; it remained uncommon for women even to wear blouses and skirts of different colors until the nineteenth century. Indeed, we still have a sensitivity to "seaminess" and the seamy side of things, the latter deriving from Emilia's remark to Iago about a malicious gossip "that turn'd your wit the seamy side without" (*Othello*, iv.ii). Again, there seems to have been a biblical source for this. The Gospel of John relates that, when Christ was taken down from the cross and his garments divided among the soldiers, it was seen that "his tunic was without seam [αραΦος, the only appearance of this word in the Greek New Testament], woven from top to bottom" (John 19.23). The cathedral of Trier and the parish church of Argenteuil have both claimed possession of this Holy Coat, or *tunica inconsutilis*, from the twelfth century onwards. Indeed, traditions associated with the latter claim that it is identical with the garment worn by Jesus, which was woven by the Virgin Mary, and miraculously grew with him.[11]

Although there were a number of mixed fabrics in common use in the late sixteenth and seventeenth centuries, there was also a survival of the medieval uneasiness about mixing different kinds of fabric in the same garment, which itself derived from the Levitican instruction that "neither shall there come upon thee a garment of two kinds of stuff mingled together" (Revised Standard Version, Leviticus, 19.19). Indeed, the King James Bible specifies the fabrics themselves, instructing "neither shall a garment mingled of linen and woollen come upon thee." One of the commonest of such fabrics was "linsey-woolsey," a term that arose in the late fifteenth century to describe a textile material of mixed wool and flax, and later used to refer to a dress material of coarse wool woven on to a cotton warp. The preacher Henry Smith reported in his *Preparative to Marriage* (1591) that "God forbad the people to weare linsey wolsey, because it was a sign of inconstancie."[12] The term also came to be used to describe any foolish or nonsensical mingling. "What linsie wolsy hast thou to speak to us again?" we hear in Shakespeare's *All's Well That Ends Well* (iv.i. 13). John Taylor uses the term to denounce the work of a contemporary, promising that "Such Motley, Medley, Linsy-Woolsey speeches/Would sure have made thee vilify thy breeches."[13] The mixing of fabrics also governs John Cleveland's colorful evocation of the "Linsie-Woolsie Vestry-men" who made up the mixed Parliament of the 1640s: "strange *Grottesco* this, the Church and States/(Most divine tick-tack) in a pye-bald crew."[14]

The term "motley" was used throughout the seventeenth century, not just to denote the foolish, but more generally as an image of the disorderly or vacuous. There seems to have been a particularly strong association between empty, vain or pretentious language and the wearing of motley. In 1611, John Davies wrote a poem called "Paper's Complaint," in which he has his vocal paper protest against the triviality of the events with which chroniclers "Do so absurdly sableize my White," complaining that such frivolity "spotteth mee/With Medley of their Mottled Liverie."[15] The vacuously imitative courtier was often identified as a wearer of motley. "Away thou fondling motley humorist," writes John Donne in his first "Satyre," preferring the "constant company" of the books in his study to the prospect that he might "follow headlong, wild uncertaine thee."[16] Donne fills this picture out in Satyre IIII, which evokes one such crossbred creature, "A thing more strange, then on Niles slime, the Sunne/E'er bred, or all which into Noahs Arke came," whose clothing matches his patched-together speech and "Pedants motley tongue."

His cloths were strage [sic]
though coarse; & black, though
bare;
Sleevelesse his jerkin was, and it
had beene
Velvet, but 'twas now (so much
ground was seene)
Become Tufftaffatie; and our
children shall
See it plaine Rashe awhile, then
nought at all.[17]

Pedantry, the piecing out of new works out of old, was also regularly seen in terms of the patchwork of motley. Thomas Dekker calls down the curse of the Muses on "thin-headed fellowes that live upon the scraps of invention" and "*Word-pirates*" so that "whatsoever they weave (in the motley-loome of their rustie pates) may like a beggers cloake, be full of stolne patches, and yet never a patch like one another."[18]

Motley is the condition of the fool, because fools were thought of as "naturals," no better than brutes in their lack of judgment or measure. The natural world tended

to be regarded as innocently motleyed. To be a "natural" was also to be no more than the clothes one wore, which, in scarcely even holding themselves together, emblematize the scattered wits of the fool. When Jacques in Shakespeare's *As You Like It* mutters "a material fool" as he listens to Touchstone's wooing of Audrey (iii.3, 28), he is playing with the meanings of "a substantial fool," as in the legal expression "a material witness" and a fool who is as flappingly insubstantial as cloth. Enid Welsford observes that fools were often also associated with the wearing or carrying of feathers, which she associates with Irish traditions that clairvoyant, wood-dwelling lunatics would turn into birds.[19]

But clothes, as opposed to plumage, belong to the order of the human; they are, at best, the sign of the natural, and thus, unnatural. To be no more than your clothes is not just to be a nothing, but the specific kind of gratuitous nothing that can be seen as the essence of the human. Calderon's 1634 play *Belshazzar's Feast* contains a fool character, the Gracioso, who makes the link between the vacuity of skin and the volatility of thought:

With a thousand colours glowing
Like to many-hued emission
The chameleon's skin gives
out . . .
*   Thus strangely wrought*
Restless, rapid, on I fly,
Nothing, everything am I,
Since I am the Human Thought.[20]

The very familiarity of the idea of mindless motley, along with the increasingly knowing appearance of

fools in drama, started to turn the simple and reliable sign of motley into a sign that was itself complex or mottled, in that it was uncertain whether it was sign or mere stuff—material witness or just material. The figure of Dissimulation is described in Robert Wilson's 1584 play *Three Ladies of London* as "having on a farmers long coat, and a cappe, and powle and beard painted motley,"[21] and Edward Guilpin complained in 1598 that "motley fac'd Dissimulation,/Is crept into our every fashion."[22]

Patching

The increasing affluence, social mobility, and migration that helped bring about from the sixteenth century onwards the liberation of fashion from the uniform signification of occupation or degree also made it possible for styles like motley to develop a special kind of allure. One sign of this is the capacity to play with the negativity of motley, most notably in the remarkable fashion for "patching" that held sway in Europe from the 1590s to at least the 1720s. Like so many fashions, it was believed to have been brought back to England from France. "What is there in Fraunce to be learnd more than in England?" growled Thomas Nashe in his *Unfortunate Traveller* of 1594. "I have knowen some that have continued there by the space of half a dozen yeare, and when they come home . . . Nought else have they profited by their travell, save learnt to . . . weare a velvet patch on their face, and walke melancholy with their armes folded."[23] By 1604, Thomas Dekker and John Webster have the character of Judith in their play

Westward Hoe, resolving that "when als done, I must follow his counsell, and take a patch, I have had one long ere this, but for disfiguring my face: yet I had noted that a masticke patch upon some womens Temples hath bin the very rheuwme of beauty."[24] The patch was sometimes known as a "moucheron," or "little fly" defined by Randle Cotgrave's *Dictionarie of the French and English Tongues* of 1611 as "*the little blacke patch thats glued by Masticke, &c, on the faces of many.*"[25] Women would apply dark patches of fabric to their faces, perhaps originally to cover blemishes and pockmarks, but increasingly because of the power to fascinate that they seemed to gather on their own terms. The coyest and most subtle of these would mimic moles, to the explication of which many popular fortune-telling books and pamphlets were devoted during the seventeenth and eighteenth centuries. But patching could also display the epidemic tendency that we have seen is so frequently associated with spots. Not surprisingly, patching became associated with prostitution and pox.[26]

Thereafter the practice of spotting or patching is regularly denounced in the Puritan literature against the extremes of ostentation in female dress that flourished both before the Civil War and in the Restoration. "Why Oyles? Waters for Teeth? Why void of Grace?/With spots (like *Rats-Dung*) to blacke patch the face? . . . Why wrong Heav'ns work-manship, with such hie sin?" demanded Nathaniel Richards in his (vicious) 1630 poem, "The Vicious Courtier," concluding that "The painted outside of a tempting Face,/Spotted with Hell, stands sequestred from Grace."[27] A pamphlet of 1665, written in the thick of a serious outbreak of the plague in London, accused those who wore patches of being harbingers of pestilence.[28] The most sustained assault upon the patching craze of what it calls "the spotted Generation" is to be found in a pamphlet entitled *A Wonder of Wonders* of 1662, by "Miso-Spilus."[29]

In his *Anthropometamorphosis, or The Artificial Changeling* of 1650, John Bulwer offers a rather more reasoned consideration of the practice, as part of his review of the curious customs of adornment and bodily modification practiced by barbarous peoples across the world:

> *Our English Ladies, who seem to have borrowed many of the Cosmetical conceits from barbarous Nations, are seldome known to be contented with a Face of Gods making . . . Sometimes they want a Mole to set off their beauty, such as Venus had; then it is well if one Black-patch will serve to make their Faces remarkable, for some fill their Visages full of them, varied into all manner of shapes and figures, which is as odious and as senseless an affectation as ever was used by any barbarous Nation in the world.*[30]

Bulwer does his best to try to account for the fascination of the patch. Ladies who patch are mistaken, he says, in their adherence to the principle of intensification by contrast, namely that "contraries compared and placed neere one another shew their lustre more plainly," such that "imperfection can make perfect" (156–7). This was a common justification in a period that was as fascinated by contrariety as it professed to be unnerved by it. A song by Henry Bold affirms that "The choice Grace/Of a Face/By a black Patch, out-set is:/The best Stone,/Fairest she'wn,/Within a foile of Jet is."[31] A poem by Robert Heath written in praise of the mole on his mistress's cheek voices similar sentiments:

How fair a Character hath Nature wrot!
 And printed on her cheek in black and white!
While this i' th' fairer Copie is no blot,
 But a ful period; that the Reader might
The better understand the sence, and know
 That here Shee stopt, and could no further go.[32]

Bulwer will have none of these arguments of perfection wrought from blemish. A spotted face pleases rather "because it gives envy satisfaction, which takes pleasure in defects, or by reason it takes away that astonishment, which instead of delighting confounds" (p. 157). Having rejected the explanation of the spot's allure based upon the intensification of beauty, Bulwer then offers an alternative argument based upon the dynamics of viewing in the spectator:

For these Spots in a beautiful Face, adde not grace to a Visage, nor increase delight; they entertain it, because they

extinguish, and then renew it. Our natural power is limited to a certain measure; when the continual presence of the delightful object doth exceed, the delight ceases, and coming to the extream of what it can contribute, it delights no longer: He that will renew his pleasure must begin with pain, and go out of the natural state to return into it; Let him look upon the Spots, then return to behold the beauty of the Face. (p. 157)

The argument uses a proto-Freudian model of the economics of sensation. The idea seems to be that, having reached an unsustainable maximum, followed by inevitable diminishment, the pleasure principle may reassert itself in replenished form. The temporary contemplation of the unpleasurable can similarly intensify pleasure. The distinction that Bulwer is attempting to make here is a subtle one. Indeed, there seems little to choose between this argument and the one that he intends to displace. Shifting attention as he does from the object of contemplation to the contemplator serves simply to explain the operations whereby beauty is indeed intensified by contrast. The interest of Bulwer's tangled reasoning lies in the fact that he acknowledges that there is indeed a pleasure in the spotted, a pleasure that seems in some complex way entangled with the apparent balking of the pleasure principle.

The career of the patch was long, though there are signs that it was also intermittent enough for some of its comebacks to be surprising.

Pepys records what seems to have been his first sight of women sporting "black spots" on 14 May 1660. His account of a conversation with the up-and-coming Lord Sandwich, on 20 October of that year suggests that it was once again becoming the fashion at court: "he was very merry and did talk very high how he would have a French Cooke and a Master of his Horse, and his lady and child to wear black patches." A few weeks later, on 4 November, Pepys was writing "My wife seemed very pretty today, it being the first time I have given her leave to weare a black patch."[33] A certain suspicion always clung to the patch or spot, which hovered between the conditions of a pastiche and a covering for a real blemish. On 5 May 1668, Pepys records seeing the Lady Castlemayne effecting what seem like running repairs by means of a patch at the theater: she called to one of her women, another that sat by this, for a little patch off her face, and put it into her mouth and wetted it and so clapped it upon her own by the side of her mouth. I suppose "she feeling a pimple rising there."[34] Beauty and infirmity were always in close vicinity in the patch. A poem of a few years later mocks its patched subject in these terms:

Why then in plain, 'tis a blot in your Scutchin.
Which we must not a patch, but plaister call,
Not bought at Change but beg'd at th' Hospital.
Nor dost thou patch, but botch.

Under these circumstances, it is no longer clear what is foil and what is jewel, as the ground expands to become the figure:

> *Why dost thou finger 't so? and keep a coil,*
> *To trim a face that is itself a foil.*
> *Indeed I question which the foil wou'd be,*
> *The leporous looks, or rusty taffitie.*[35]

The extent to which the addiction to patching could go is indicated by a story told by the seventeenth-century gentleman scientist Kenelm Digby. He describes a kinswoman of his who was quite unable to show herself in public without a rash of black patches, in the shape of stars and crescents, stuck on her face and neck. When she became pregnant, Digby warned her of the danger of transmitting the marks to the countenance of her child, suggesting that the patches might even coalesce to form one large unsightly blotch. His alarmed kinswoman abandoned her beloved patches, but the effect of brooding on the damage she might already have caused was enough, Digby tells us, to ensure that when her baby was born, it did indeed bear a large dark mark on its forehead.[36]

Digby's story forms part of the extensive literature from the sixteenth century onwards on the power of mothers to transmit birthmarks to their unborn children as a result of alarm or unrequited longing (birthmarks used to be called "longing marks" and are still called *envies* in French). He tells this story as part of a proof of the magical sympathies that exist between objects and persons and the possibility of effects at a

distance. The fact that spots could spread not just across a body, but between bodies, as the effect simply of impulse or imagination, makes spots the touch of another in one's most intimate being; spots come *from elsewhere*. The fact that Digby was an atomist, who explained the transmission of such images and marks by means of the fact that bodies are continually giving off impalpable films and species of atoms, which then mingle with other bodies, suggests the apprehension of an infinitesimal spottedness or particulation at the very heart of things.

Pied Beauty
By spotting their flesh with fabric, these ladies (and sometimes gentlemen) were inverting the normal condition of things. The spot seems to be the formal antagonist of woven fabrics, since it represents the puncturing or unravelling of the reciprocally supporting lines and reticulations that form the structure of the fabric. The spot is the fly, not so much in the ointment, as struggling against the web. Clothing and decorative fabrics have therefore often followed the astrological impulse by generally avoiding the use of irregular spots, or attempted to regularize their spacing and disposition, thus bending the alogic of the spot to the more predictable topography of the line, and restoring the levelness and continuity of the surface that an irregularly spotted pattern seems to compromise.

The principle governing many apparently spotted patterns is that they should be subtly educated and controlled by lines or stripes, which provide as it were the supporting stave for their dots and quavers—for example in many of the more delicate Laura Ashley wallpapers and fabrics. It is as though it were the principle of weave itself which were being maintained or reasserted through this gridwork. Where spots are not being chivvied in this way into lines and rectangles, they can be neutralized by distance. Questions of scale and magnitude seem to be important here. One must either be brought up close enough to spotted patterns to be able to make out clearly the contours of the rose, the jewel, the eye, the head, of which the spot is formed, or the pattern must be held back from us sufficiently that the eye cannot resolve the busy sizzle of the surface into its separate elements. The latter would seem to be the case, for example, both in *pointilliste* painting, and also in designs like the "shower-of-hail" overcoat, the descendant of Elizabethan mixed motley. Indeterminate patterns of spots can also be used, somewhat more dubiously, to camouflage, as in kitchen linoleum, or flecked carpet. It will be a long time, one can surmise, before spots gain the reputation for being hygienic that stripes have done, which is why spotted underpants can be worn only as a joke.

The clustering together of small spots not only neutralizes the question asked of the surface by the spot, it also conjures from the venomous powers of the spotted a mildly intoxicant effect. Dots can be dizzying (as when one "sees stars" or gets "spots before the eyes"), but because of this, they can be frivolous, playful, pleasantly narcotic.

This seems to be part of the reason that spots have been associated from the nineteenth century onwards with bedroom fabrics: with pyjamas, bed-hangings, and quilts. Spotted or irregular patterns that mildly disconcert seem to have the effect of dulling attention and thereby encouraging sleep. Anything more definite, or more easily brought into focus, might constitute an inducement to hallucination or disturbed sleep, suggested Robert Edis in his *Decoration and Furniture of Town Houses*.[37]

And yet, since the curious habit of patching complexions in order to show them more fair took hold in the seventeenth century, the spotted has steadily grown in fascination and prestige. Spots are subject to what Barbara Maria Stafford has called the exoticizing tendency apparent in Europe from the end of the Enlightenment onwards, whereby whatever is regarded as strange, disorderly or singular can become aesthetically valued.[38] That preference for the fragment over the whole that Nietzsche believed predominated in eras of decadence can be found in the growing tolerance of motley, spottedness, and inconstancy in Baudelaire, while a somewhat dangerous delight in spottedness is to be found in Oscar Wilde's *Picture of Dorian Gray*, in which a particularly exquisite orchid is described as "a marvelous spotted thing, as effective as the seven deadly sins." The love of what is brindled, freaked, and streaked is particularly intense in the work of Gerard Manley Hopkins, who found many ways to declare the glory of "dappled things," and of "All things

counter, original, spare, strange;/Whatever is fickle, freckled (who knows how?)/With swift, slow; sweet, sour; adazzle, dim."[39]

The ambivalence of spottedness is in large degree the expression of human ambivalence about nature. Admiration of nature's variety and abundance can often be expressed in terms of an appreciation of the spotted. Certainly speckledness and spottedness have long been valued by breeders of livestock, and collectors of birds'-eggs, while spotted fawns and speckled trout are signs of natural delicacy and abundance. That this preference has a long lineage is indicated by the story of Jacob's ruse to induce his cattle to give birth to spotted and streaked offspring (*Genesis* 30:30–43). A greyhound with a white spot on its forehead has been regarded as lucky among Welsh racegoers, and a special respect is reserved for dappled horses.[40] The refrain "I've lost my spotted cow" in the English folk song "The Spotted Cow," which indicates the loss of cowherd's maidenhead, suggests the prizing of the spotted. In fact, the preference for spotted or mottled nature may be stronger among humans, or at least those in the West, than in nature itself, for patterns of breeding in the wild tend to produce much more uniformity than among domesticated animals.

The fact that prinked, prickled or freckled patterns became associated with inattention and irresponsibility means that spots have developed markedly childish connotations. More even than to the bedroom, spots nowadays belong to the nursery (or to that outdoor, adult nursery, the beach). All over the world, children learning to read are now beguiled by the adventures of a puppy called, simply, "Spot." The well-established link between childishness and femininity means that spots and dots have much more distinctively female associations than stripes—a banker can wear a striped tie with ease, but a man who comes into the office with a spotted tie still risks being thought of as a fop, an oaf or an exhibitionist. But it is the circus that has done most of the work of quarantining the spot by exaggeration. Clowns, with their lugubriously maculated eyes, oozing fat teardrops, their great ruby noses, the perfect disks of red worn on their cheeks, the balloon-like circles that bloom over their costumes, are spottedness at once run riot and fixed in place by magnification and geometrization. Episodes of willing or sanctioned clownishness, like the "Red Nose" days operated by the British charity Comic Relief, similarly license a kind of spottedness in order to hold it at bay.

The polka dot represents the most conspicuous triumph of the spot over cultural mistrust—or rather, perhaps, the triumph of that mistrust over the spot. The origins of the name are obscure, but it seems to be the only survivor of the practice of naming products after the craze for the polka that swept across Europe and, more especially, America during the 1870s and 1880s. Polka dots have maintained their position partly as a result of the growing tolerance for, and commodification of childishness or harmless, irresponsible cuteness in the modern world. Brian Hyland's 1960 hit song "Itsy Bitsy Teenie Weenie Yellow Polka Dot Bikini" continued the tradition of making sexuality safe with babytalk. A website currently advertising a range of pretty ribbons and boxes urges its customers "with a splash of whimsy and a touch of fun, add a sparkle with dainty polka dots." But the polka dot defends against the indeterminacy lurking in the spot by its perfect circularity and the clear differentiation it makes between foreground and background. The heyday of the polka dot was during the 1960s, when it multiplied on miniskirts, handbags, shoes, hats and other accessories, sometimes roughed up a little, for example into the "leopardskin pillbox hat" of which Bob Dylan sang so sneeringly on his *Blonde on Blonde* album. During the 1970s, the polka dots of mod fashion bred unpredictably with the spirals of hippie typography, the swirling splotches of tie-dyed T-shirts, and ubiquitous faux-Celtic curlicues. Everywhere one looked, straight lines were being coiled over on themselves or flooded with dabs and daubs of color. For all of the alleged anarchism and dissidence of punk, the challenge of its iconography depended on the reassertion of the disciplinary power of the stripe, the tear, the slash, the bar sinister, the diagonal, and the zigzag.

I have said that there is always a kind of premonition in the spotted. The current universality of the image formed of dots, and the fascination with its construction, for example in the printing of T-shirts with fuzzy newspaper-quality images suggests that perhaps the long-established authority of the textile metaphor of the world as network is beginning to be surpassed, in favor of the patchy, pluralized, parti-colored mosaic of a world. Michel Serres evokes the knowledge needed to apprehend such a world at the beginning of his *Le Tiers-instruit*, translated as *The Troubadour of Knowledge*. He imagines Harlequin, newly returned from his journey to the moon, denying that there is any difference between it and the earth, but being betrayed by the very form of his cape, which is "[a] motley composite made of pieces, of rags or scraps of every size, in a thousand forms and different colors, of varying ages, from different sources, badly basted, inharmoniously juxtaposed, with no attention paid to proximity, mended according to need, accident, and contingency."[41] Harlequin responds to the jeers of the crowd by removing his cape, only to reveal another, just the same, and then "another colorfully patterned body stocking spotted like an ocelot," and beneath that, a skin covered in tattoos that reproduce his many coats, maculate and patched.[42] This world, a world deep as the skin, and as motley, is one in which, as William James put it, "there is no bedding; it is as if the pieces clung together by their edges, the transitions between them forming their cement:"[43] a spotty, turbulent, now-you-see-it, now-you-don't world, that is not so much falling as coming to bits.

Notes

1. Michel Pastoureau, *The Devil's Cloth: A History of Stripes and Striped Clothing*, trans. Jody Gladding (New York: Columbia University Press, 2001), pp. 13–14, 55–61.

2. Saul Nathaniel Brody, *The Disease of the Soul: Leprosy in Medieval Literature* (Ithaca NY and London: Cornell University Press, 1974), p. 51.

3. Robert Henryson, *The Poems*, ed. Denton Fox (Oxford: Clarendon Press, 1987), pp. 113, 122.

4. Philip Sidney, *The Countess of Pembrokes Arcadia*, 2nd edn (London: John Windet for William Ponsonbie, 1593), Bk 1, p. 33.

5. Michel Pastoureau, "Formes et couleurs du désordre: le jaune avec le vert," *Médiévales* 4 (1983): 62–73.

6. Guido Kisch, "The Yellow Badge in History," *Historia Judaica* 19 (1957), p. 104.

7. "Taliban Defends Hindu Badges Plan," Guardian 24 May, 2001: http://www.guardian.co.uk/ international/story/ 0,3604,495531,00.html

8. Enid Welsford, *The Fool: His Social and Literary History* (1935; London: Faber & Faber, 1968), pp. 121–4, 334.

9. Leslie Hotson, *Shakespeare's Motley* (1952; New York: Haskell House, 1971), pp. 33–43.

10. Ibid., p. 100.

11. J. N. Rutland, *Von der Verehrung der Reliquien im Allgemeinen und der des heiligen Rockes zu Trier insbesondere* (Berlin, 1844); Gabriel Gerberon, *L'histoire de la robe sans couture de . . . Jesus Christ, qui est revereée dans l'Eglise du Monastere des Religieux Benedictins d'Argenteüil. Avec un abregé l'histoire de ce monastere* (Paris, 1677).

12. Henry Smith, *A Preparative to Marriage* (London: Thomas Orwin for Thomas Man, 1591), p. 157.

13. John Taylor, "Taylors Revenge: Or, The Rimer William Fennor, Firkt, Ferrited, and finely Fetcht over the Coales," *All The Workes of Iohn Taylor, The Water Poet* (London: for James Boler, 1630), p. 147.

14. John Cleveland, "The Mixt Assembly," *The Character of a London-Diurnall* (London, 1647), p. 29.

15. John Davies, "Papers Complaint, Compild in Ruthfull Rimes," *The Scourge of Folly . . .* (London: Edward Allde for R. Redmer, 1611), p. 238.

16. John Donne, "Satyre 1," *Poems* (London: John Marriot, 1633), p. 326.

17. John Donne, "Satyre IIII," ibid., pp. 338–9.

18. Thomas Dekker, "To The Reader," *The Wonderfull Yeare. 1603* (London: Thomas Creede for N. Ling, J. Smethwick and J. Browne, 1603), A3ᵛ–A4ʳ.

19. Welsford, *The Fool: His Social and Literary History* (1935; London, Faber & Faber, 1968), pp. 97–9.

20. Pedro Calderón de la Barca, *Belshazzar's Feast* (1634), *Mysteries of Corpus Christi*, trans. Denis Florence MacCarthy (Dublin: James Duffy, 1867), pp. 121–3.

21. Robert Wilson, *A Right Excellent and Famous Comoedy Called The Three Ladies of London* (London: by Roger Warde, 1584), Act 2, sig. Aiiᵛ.

22. Edward Guilpin, "Satyra Prima," *Skialetheia: Or a shadowe of Truth in certaine Epigrams and Satyres* (London: for Nicholas Ling, 1598), sig. C4ʳ.

23. Thomas Nashe, *The Unfortunate Traveller: Or, The Life of Jack*

Wilton, 2nd edn (London: Thomas Scarlet for Cuthbert Burby, 1594), p. 85.

24. Thomas Dekker and John Webster, *Westward Hoe* (London: for John Hodges *et al.*, 1607), Act 2.1, sig. C1^r.

25. Randle Cotgrave, *A Dictionarie of the French and English Tongues* (London: Adam Islip, 1611), sig. Hhh5^v.

26. N. F. Lowe, "Hogarth, Beauty Spots and Sexually-Transmitted Diseases," *British Journal for Eighteenth-Century Studies* 15 (1992): 71–9.

27. Nathaniel Richards, "The Vicious Courtier," *The Celestiall Publican . . .* (London: Felix Kyngston for Roger Michell, 1630), sigs H2^v–H3^r. Patching is also condemned in Thomas Hall's *Comarum ακοσμια: the loathesomeness of long haire . . . with the concurrent judgement of divines both old and new against it. With an appendix against painting, spots, naked breasts, etc.* (London: 1654).

28. *The Prophecie of One Of His Maiesties Chaplains, Concerning the Plague, and Black-Patches* (London: for G. Horton, 1665), p. 2.

29. *A Wonder of Wonders: or; a metamorphosis of fair faces voluntarily transformed into foul visages. Or, an invective against black-spotted faces: by a well-wisher to modest matrons and virgins, Miso-Spilus i. qui maculis odit* (London: 'Published by R. Smith, Gent.': J. G. for Richard Royston, 1662), p. 8.

30. John Bulwer, *Anthropometamorphosis; Man Transform'd; or, The Artifflcial Changeling. Historically Presented in the mad and cruel Gallantry, Foolish Bravery, ridiculous Beauty, Filthy Finenesse, and loathesome Lovelinesse of most NATIONS, Fashioning & altering their Bodies from the Mould intended by NATURE . . .* (London: for J. Hardesty, 1650), p. 156. References in my text hereafter.

31. Henry Bold, "Song LX: A Round, at the Request of Sir W. B.," in *Poems: Lyrique, Macaronique, Heroique, &c* (London: for Henry Brome, 1664), p. 96.

32. Robert Heath, "On a Black Mole on Clarastella's Faire Check," *Clarastella: Together With Poems Occasional, Elegies, Epigrams, Satyrs* (London: for Humph. Moseley, 1650), p. 10

33. *The Diary of Samuel Pepys*, ed. Robert Latham and William Matthews, 10 vols (London: Bell and Hyman, 1983), vol. 1, pp. 139, 269, 283.

34. Ibid., vol. 9, p. 186.

35. Matthew Stevenson, "Upon a Rusty Patch on An Iron Face," *Poems, Or A Miscellany of Sonnets, Satyrs, Drollery, Panegyricks, Elegies, etc.* (London: for R. Reynolds and John Lutton, 1673), p. 71.

36. Kenelm Digby, *A Late Discourse Made in a Solemn Assembly of Noble and Learned Men at Montpellier in France . . . Touching the Cure of Wounds By the Power of Sympathy*, trans. R. White (London: for R. Lowndes and T. Davies, 1658), pp. 101–8.

37. Robert Edis, *Decoration and Furniture of Town Houses: A Series of Cantor Lectures*, 2nd

edn (London: Kegan Paul & Co., 1881).

38. Barbara Maria Stafford, *Body Criticism: Imaging the Unseen in Enlightenment Art and Medicine* (Cambridge, MA and London: MIT Press, 1991), pp. 329–39.

39. Gerard Manley Hopkins, "Pied Beauty," *Poems of Gerard Manley Hopkins*, 4th edn, ed. W. H. Gardner and N. H. Mackenzie (London: Oxford University Press, 1970), p. 70.

40. Philippa Waring, *A Dictionary of Omens and Superstitions* (London: Souvenir Press, 1978), p. 111; Francis Haines, *Appaloosa: The Spotted Horse in Art and History* (Austin, TX: University of Texas Press, 1963).

41. Michel Serres, *The Troubadour of Knowledge*, trans. Sheila Faria Glaser and William Paulson (Ann Arbor: University of Michigan Press, 1997), pp. xiii–xiv.

42. Ibid., p. xv.

43. William James, "A World of Pure Experience," in *Essays on Radical Empiricism* (1912; Lincoln, NE and London: University of Nebraska Press, 1996), p. 86.

Domesticating the Exotic: Floral Culture and the East India Calico Trade with England, c. 1600–1800

Abstract

Europe's burgeoning trade in the seventeenth century brought exciting new textiles from Asia to the west, at the same time as newly imported flora caused a frenzy among botanists, collectors, gardeners and speculators. Between 1600 and 1800, gardens were reconceived; at the same time, interior domestic spaces were also being redesigned. Imagined landscapes of exotic locales became the inspiration for a redesign of personal settings using the painted, printed textiles from India. The fervor tied to the romance, mystery and alien landscapes of Asia unleashed a decorative torrent in thread, silk and linen, to bedeck the walls and furnish the homes of elite and common citizens. Asian-inspired dress also held a particular fascination for men from the middling to elite ranks, who were beguiled by the decorative banyans or dressing gowns made of printed and painted silks and cottons. They chose to wear these loose flowered robes as they socialized with their most intimate friends and family. Over two centuries, calicos became domesticated, a permanent feature of English domestic furnishings and personal adornment, a symbol of genteel repose, of male informality and intimacy, evolving to become a constant component of western material culture and thereby refashioning the domestic world.

BEVERLY LEMIRE

Beverly Lemire is Professor of History and University Research Professor at the University of New Brunswick, Canada. Her books include, *Fashion's Favourite: the Cotton Trade and the Consumer in Britain* (Oxford, 1991) and *Dress, Culture and Commerce: the English Clothing Trade before the Factory* (Basingstoke, 1997). She is the incoming co-editor of *Textile History* and has articles published in that journal as well as in journals such as *Continuity and Change, Dress, Costume, Journal of Social History* and *Journal of British Studies*.

Textile, Volume 1, Issue 1, pp. 65–85
Reprints available directly from the Publishers.
Photocopying permitted by licence only.

Domesticating the Exotic: Floral Culture and the East India Calico Trade with England, *c.* 1600–1800

Adam Smith recognized that he lived in an era shaped by two great milestones—in his words: "The discovery of America, and that of a passage to the East Indies by the Cape of Good Hope, are the two greatest and most important events recorded in the history of mankind."[1] The realignment of world trading markets through a developing European hegemonic system, with a routine exchange of commodities, reshaped East and West and has been the focus of intensive study in recent years.[2] Contact between Europe and Asia, between Western consumer markets and diverse foreign societies, reshaped European perceptions of the world and their place within this panoply of marvels. Sixteenth- and seventeenth-century European collectors reveled in the accumulation of exotics, as Asian manufacturers altered their products to suit European tastes.[3] Within a century the trade goods from Asia included both matchless artifacts and mass-market commodities, goods with which we are all familiar: ceramics, japanned ware, metal goods, silks, painted cottons, and printed calicos. Ultimately, these imports helped produce a new conceptualization of Englishness, concepts reinforced through a more complex material culture and practice. My focus will be on Indian painted and printed cottons, one of the most noteworthy of the new commodities. What accounted for the insatiable demand for these wares? Why was there such an enthusiastic reception from such a broad range of plebeian and elite men and women? Many contemporaries, reeling from the economic shock of the mass of Asian imports, alleged that it was the cheap price of Indian cottons that secured their place in European markets.[4] However, economic considerations alone cannot explain the impact of these textiles. In this paper I will briefly summarize the dimensions of the calico trade and consider the conjunction of events that converted these flowered commodities from exotic to staple; I will also speculate on the impulses within English and European societies that fed the passion for calicos and chintzes and trace the ways in which these East Indian textiles transformed the domestic environment; for the flood of Asian floral draperies reshaped the material idioms of English life, framing new cultural and economic patterns visible to this day.

Bengals, and Silks, of Indian Making[5]

No sooner did the Portuguese establish regular voyages to the East Indies than they identified one of the most desirable manufactures of the Indian subcontinent, the painted, printed, and embroidered fabrics of that region. Spices originally lured Europeans to find a sea route to Asia, but textiles quickly became one of the important staples and very soon large cargos were assembled annually to meet Western demand. The Indian textile industry was ancient at the time of contact with these traders, experienced in serving markets from China to Persia to Africa long before Western traders arrived on the scene. However, Indian merchants were as willing to trade with these new Western seafarers as with their more familiar foreign customers. The goods they offered in cottons and silks were unrivaled in variety, arrayed in breath-taking shades and seductive patterns, with stylized motifs of the flora and fauna little known in Europe, many incorporating patterns brought to India from within their trading network, further enriching the styles available for sale. Embroidered quilts were sold in Portugal by the 1520s[6] and embroidered calico garments were owned by members of Philip II's household as gradually the floral forms of Indian calicos became a recognizable fashion among the Iberian nobility. Slowly, inexorably these goods spread among elite buyers dazzled by the novelty of these floral embellished textiles; circulating through the Hapsburg trading network, they arrived on England's southern shores about the mid-sixteenth century.

English households were in transition, inside and outside, as bourgeois housing gradually became more substantial, comfortable and decorative. The spread and interpretation of these changes among householders varied with their geography, as well as social rank and personal disposition, as Lorna Weatherill observed in her later study of domestic material culture from 1660 to 1760. Weatherill also opined that the, "consumption of many household goods increased before 1725 and continued to do so afterwards."[7] There was a continuum in the momentum of consumer purchases and consumer goods. Not surprisingly, changes in the late sixteenth and early seventeenth century were influenced even more sharply by proximity and accessibility to new commodities at a time when national markets were still to be developed and regional imperatives shaped the character of consumer spending. The port of Southampton was ideally situated for the early introduction of novelties, being open to trade from continental Europe and beyond. Innovations included the purchase of a range of new household accoutrements, as William Harrison observed of his Hampshire neighbors in 1577:

the furniture of our houses also exceedeth and is grown in manner even to passing delicacy; and herein I do not speak of the nobility and gentry only but likewise of the lowest sort in most places of our South Country that have anything at all to take to . . . in the houses of knights, gentlemen, merchantmen, and some other wealthy citizens, it is not . . . [uncommon] to behold generally their great provision of tapestry, Turkey work, pewter, brass, fine linen, and . . . lower even unto the inferior artificers and many farmers, who . . . have for the most part learned also to garnish their cupboards with plate, their joint beds with tapestry and silk hangings, and their tables with carpets and fine napery.[8]

Decades before the formal organization of the English East India Company, the English appetite for textile rarities from the East Indies was in evidence. Probate inventories from Southampton confirm the presence of Indian imports both in the houses of local citizens and in the stock of local merchants, a testament to the speed with which these commodities were introduced. As one of the major ports, Southampton had the wealth to attract the widest array of foreign products, of which Asian goods were the newest arrivals, adding to the complexity and diversity of domestic decor. In 1559, the widow Margaret Pyd included calico curtains among her possessions on her death. John Smith's extensive list of goods revealed a well-furnished house including a "Cubborde clothe of Callycowe"—the value of this item was a fraction of the value of the "Carpett for a Cubbarde of Venys worke" that he also owned. The grocer John Staveley had a similarly elaborate household, including three calico cushions among his assortment of linens. The records from this period show that these Asian wares were part of a myriad of European niceties and luxuries owned by Southampton's elite including a

Spanish chair, numerous Venice carpets, "Flanders worke payntyd wth frames," and a walnut chest. Amidst the steady flow of useful and luxurious merchandise were included the newest textiles from Asia, embellished not according to any existing European techniques, such as through fine brocade or tapestry weaving, but with the vibrant dyes, sinuous painting styles and distinctive floral devices synonymous with the Indian subcontinent. Seven years later, in 1566, a gentleman of Southampton numbered more calico cushions among his possessions at death, though these were described as "olde" by his executors. To John Norton, the lengths of calico in his possession were valuable enough to be specially noted in his will as a bequest to a relative in 1568: "2 furred gowns, a new felt of Spain that hath not been worn, and 4 black skins of Spain. 7 ells of calico—3 ells of the finer piece and 4 of the coarse piece." At his death in 1573, the merchant Reynold Howse held ten pieces of calico among his considerable stocks of fabrics, lace, ribbons, thread and accessories. And, in the same year, Richard Goddard, a merchant of Poole, included ten pieces of fine and coarse calico among his stock, while in his house he had positioned a calico cupboard cloth in his hallway.[9] This probate evidence suggests the steady trickle of East Indian merchandise seeping in to southern England, goods with an instant appeal to men and women. In 1615, for example, the vogue for these items inspired Lady Arundel to purchase sets of curtains to complement her "bedde of Japan," while the Earl of Northumberland showed off a number of what he called "China quilts" by 1614; all testifying to the instant and enthusiastic response to these Asian wares.[10] Thus at least some of England's aspiring ladies and gentlemen, nobles and commoners, had not had to await the creation of an East India Company in England in order to acquire the newest fabric fashions.

Trade links with Spanish and Portuguese merchants spread these goods through northern Europe and laid the groundwork for even more extensive imports, once English merchants began to ply the waters of the Indian Ocean after 1600. In the seventeenth century, at the time of growing contact with European trading companies, the Indian subcontinent was the largest producer of cotton textiles in the world—Indian merchants were easily able to adapt their products to suit European tastes, much as they had for other foreign markets. With the formalization of trade links, bales of textiles followed the quilts to European ports, with colors and designs customized for Western buyers at the direction of European merchants.[11] Between 1664 and 1678, the value of the English East India Company textile imports averaged between 60% and 70% of their trade, with more than one million pieces imported in 1684.[12] Writing to India in 1691, the Directors of the English company noted that "You can send us nothing amiss at this time when everything of India is so much wanted."[13]

Floral Culture and the Calico Trade

I have described elsewhere the intense efforts of the English East

India Companies to constrain cost and ensure quality and variety among their imported textiles; price played a major role in the penetration of chintz and calicos into ever-wider markets. In fact, for one brief period, the flood of inexpensive calicos were even cheaper than linen goods.[14] But if price was an important factor for the middle- and lower-level markets, price alone does not explain the extraordinary appeal of calico and chintz. The passion for East Indian textiles was excited by another powerful cultural factor—the fascination with all things floral, the enchantment with flowers and botany that swirled from elite and academic circles to the flower pots on garret window sills and the flowered hangings on plaster walls. In his insightful study *The Culture of Flowers*, Jack Goody observes that on the question of flowers

> *there have been important changes over time, influenced by the growth of botany, the uses of written knowledge and literature, the nature of leisure, the arts of reproduction, by modes of production and by more immediate concerns . . . For in taking the subject of flowers, we are already dealing with the domesticated as well as the wild, with images or representation as well as "reality" or what is represented, in other words, with objects and their uses that are influenced by wider sets of practices and beliefs.*

Goody is one among many who identify the period from the sixteenth to the nineteenth century, in Europe, as an era when "[t]he range of actual flowers increased enormously and flower gardens became more popular, fuelled by the advent of luxurious exotic blooms from both East and West, which followed from the expansion of European trade and colonisation."[15] At the same time as some European sea captains carried the first samples of Indian flowered fabrics back to Europe, other voyagers sought out flora from the new colonial and trading areas of Asia, Africa, North and South America, hoping these would find favor with botanists and eventually find a wider market in northern gardens. The iconic power of flowers and floral motifs is of central importance, not least for the multiple meanings assigned to plants themselves as well as floral designs, by country dwellers and city folk, by genteel scholars and middling traders. Ruth Phillips observes that, "the privileging of the floral within . . . consumer cultures must be denaturalized and historicized."[16] This said, the things so long familiar to us—chintz-covered sofas, calico curtains and floral embroidered pincushions—must be reconsidered, both their ancestry and their domestication in English settings, their contribution to the creation of Englishness in material culture and cultural idiom.

Floral designs were the hallmarks of East Indian textiles, with calicos, chintzes, muslins, and percales bedizened with sprays of blossom and verdant trees-of-life interspersed with exotic fauna. At the outset, troublesome elements in color and subject were restyled by Indian manufacturers at the behest of Western traders. But if Europeans preferred light to dark backgrounds, they were unswerving in their love for fantastical branched patterns and colorful fancies, which were demanded with all speed from Indian suppliers to meet the clamor for new goods. Commercial opportunity turned rarities into widely distributed merchandise, but voyagers pursued other goods as vigorously as Asian manufactures. Peonies, camellias, magnolias, forsythia, wisteria, and chrysanthemums traveled with china, chintz, and silk to European ports.[17] New blooming plants soon transformed the horticulture of palaces, manor houses, and city gardens. Floral culture captured the imagination of Europe, simultaneously changing exterior and interior worlds in the process.

Ana Pavord has narrated the tulip's path, from the obscurity of Turkish mountainsides to sultans' gardens, ultimately becoming the focus of a botanical and an aesthetic obsession in Europe during the early seventeenth century, giving vivid instances of the new power of flora. The early seventeenth-century tulip mania became a byword in speculative excess.[18] However, by 1635, tulip bulbs could be purchased by millers and carpenters, where just a few years ago only the wealthy could dabble in this enthusiasm.[19] Newly discovered plants were carried to Europe from the corners of the compass, soon becoming cultivated species, with blooms and colors nurtured to take novel forms, epitomizing the breadth and control over the natural world and the power of human intervention beloved by Enlightenment man. The vibrant color and seductive scent of hyacinths, the languorous beauty of peonies recalled the delights of Moorish or Mogul gardens. Raleigh Trevelyan rhapsodizes over the exquisite Alhambra, long the subject of travelers' tales: "evanescent, floating disembodied, sensuously exotic, luminous, . . . a rose preserved in snow, domes of heaven, kaleidoscope, terrestrial paradise, web of petrified lace, pearls in an emerald setting."[20] Early modern gardeners surely hoped that the glories of Islamic and Asian gardens could be recreated in northern climes, if only in part. Surely botanic wonders could be adapted and naturalized in a new setting. These hopes came to be realized as private and commercial gardens flourished and new-style flora intersected with long-held botanic practices. In England, during the Interregnum, the traditional floral symbolism incorporated in popular celebrations was quashed by Puritan forces as heathenish practice; however, the Restoration brought the end to restrictions and after 1660 garlands, floribund maypoles, and other floral festivals once again became a common feature of plebeian life. Botanical enthusiasm took on more erudite form in university settings with the establishment of the Botanic Gardens in Oxford where its advocates struggled to recreate the garden of Eden according to the precepts of the New Science.[21] By the late seventeenth century, cut flowers became a common indulgence among city folk, a phenomenon fed by the nurseries springing up on suburban fields as the culture of flowers ranged up and down the social spectrum.[22] Whether or not the intellectual

attraction to botany differed for the Oxford scholar, the Norfolk gardener or the Middlesex milkmaid, there was a shared attraction.

Garden construction abounded in England, inspired by Italian, French and Dutch interpretations of the form. The passion gripped its practitioners and one acolyte confessed as much: "I never had any other desire so strong, and so like to covetousness, as the one which I have had always, that I might be master at last of a small house and large garden, with every moderate conveniences joined to them, and there dedicate the remainder of my life only to the culture and study of nature."[23] Over the seventeenth and eighteenth centuries gardening flourished, varying in form and style according to the wealth and inclination of the gardener, from the geometric order of knot gardens to the sumptuous pleasure gardens enjoyed in public venues.[24] The English in particular rejected the formalism of continental gardens, laboring to create a natural aesthetic of landscapes, a particularly English interpretation of a reconfigured "natural" world suited to their tastes. Sir Thomas Brown celebrated the fact that in the seventeenth century, "we having China, India, and new world to supply us, beside the great distinction of flowers unknown unto antiquity, and the varieties thereof arising from art and nature."[25] John Brewer observes that, "It is as if nature had become a thing of human artifice, even a commodity." The vogue for horticulture not only resculpted the countryside into pleasing picturesque forms, it also found material expressions inside the home, as new-styled floral motifs were transcribed into domestic embellishments, as inspiration and imagination combined. As Goody reminds us, "in taking the subject of flowers, we are already dealing with the domesticated as well as the wild, . . . with objects and their uses . . . influenced by a wider set of practices and beliefs."[26]

Intimate and Exotic

Textiles are by their nature personal products; they drape the adult body and frame the wearer seductively or modestly, they swaddle at birth and shroud at death. Other colonial and Asian commodities did not touch the buyer's body so intimately, nor frame the domestic setting so visibly. Coffee, chocolate, tea, porcelain, tobacco required new ceremonial habits and a reallocation of resources to consume ephemeral, if addictive, products, or to socialize with new sorts of decorative accoutrements. These commodities certainly challenged a cultural and economic status quo.[27] However, textiles fulfilled different functions, blending the decorative with the seductive, the practical with the exotic in a unique manner, ultimately redesigning the home and redefining perceptions more personally and immediately than other colonial and Asian goods. Chronologically, there was a twinned momentum, as new flora and floral fabrics poured into Europe with the trade winds; the timing of these two phenomena coincided with one reinforcing the other. For those with land, the opportunity arose to refashion both the natural world and domestic spaces according to these new

sensibilities. But in both earth-bound and interior worlds the imagined landscapes of exotic locales became the inspiration for a redesign of personal settings and dress.

As I showed above, in the calico chronology the exotic was carried first into the home, where it gradually transformed the concept of English domestic decor. Along with calico cushions and curtains, some of the more suggestive entries in the collection of Southampton probate inventories were wall hangings, or cloths, variously described as painted or stained. In most cases there is no further description of these items, although a handful are listed with further detail, such as "stayned with bestis and fleuris".[28] These ornamental pieces were much cheaper than tapestry, painted on canvas or finer hemp or linen cloth, suggesting the wide consumer interest in decorative touches for the home. If only written records were available few other observations could arise from these probate entries. However, the Victoria and Albert Museum contains a small number of "painted cloths" dating from the seventeenth century, illustrative of the interpretive influence of East Indian motifs, even at this level of the market. These are very suggestive artifacts. Floral designs are the common themes of the three painted cloths. The first is a stiffly painted rural scene on heavy canvas with a top border of stilted flowers— if its subject matter suggests the attraction of rural settings, there is no indication that the artist's hand was guided by Indian-inspired inventions. However, in the second and third of these hangings there is

every evidence of the powerful stylistic effect of the calico trade. Both painted cloths were composed on medium-weight linen and both attempted the more fluid style of Asian painted textiles, one including bird and floral elements, the other an entirely botanic subject. In the late seventeenth century, English printers were known for their skill at imitating East Indian patterns.[29] These surviving painted hangings illustrate further examples of the effort to imitate and domesticate a powerfully attractive mode. They hint as well at the diverse markets for floral devices produced for the houses of non-elite families, carrying the representative emblems of the gardens of Asia into plebeian hallways and chambers.

In the homes of genteel families botanic imitation took other more refined forms. Fine needlework, the resort of all ladies of quality, was transformed under the influence of Indian cottons. By the early 1600s, East Indian textiles had made inroads in the bedrooms and sitting rooms of genteel and noble families, as whimsy coupled with a new design aesthetic took hold. Painted and embroidered quilts sold at a premium to discerning buyers, many with embroidered patterns typified by "thin-stalked imaginary flowers . . . embroidered over the quilting in satin stitch."[30] A 1641 letter from London to Surat explained that even at that stage "The Quilts of chints being novelties produced from £5 5s. od. to £6 the pair" adding that "a further supply therefore [is] desired, and both as regards those and the Chintz, more should be made on the white grounds, and the branches and flowers to be in collors."[31] Quilts were followed by curtains and hangings of every sort as aids to transform the common bedroom into an oriental bower. With these painted hangings the tropics were transported to northern Europe. Along with these imports came new inspirations for needlework designs, embracing all of the elements of Indian style and content. Therle Hughes considers this to have been a turning point in the history of English domestic needlework and is harshly dismissive of what he terms "the schoolgirl gaucheries of the Stuart raised stump work" which were gradually abandoned:

> *as women caught the fever to transform the major furnishings of their homes. . . . Thereafter the Indian and Anglo-Indian influence on Stuart hangings became too great to be assessed. Leaves in all their infinite variety as background detail had always appealed to tapestry and needlework designers and "forest work", "verdure" and "small leaves" hangings are to be noted from very early times in a heavy, Italianesque manner. But the patterns inspired by the Indian printed and painted cottons such as the typical tree-of-life became so wide-spread and conformed so closely in style that they have acquired the name of their period and are known merely as Jacobean. They expressed a fresh approach to the subject, altogether more fluent in line, more lively and fantastic in mood.[32]*

If the passion for gardens inspired labors of love with roots and clay, a similar fervor for the romance, mystery and alien landscapes of Asia unleashed a decorative torrent in thread, silk and linen, to bedeck the walls and appoint the homes of elite and common citizens. Asian designs, in Therle Hughes' words, "began to change still further the Englishwoman's ideas of the little fantastic worlds they created for their dreaming."[33] These imagined landscapes incorporated the fantasies of Europeans, as collections of exotic artifacts and travelers' accounts were conjoined with the motifs and stylized vistas depicted on Chinese porcelain and japanned ware. As gardens blossomed with flora of distant shores, so too private rooms underwent an efflorescence, creating a new sense of English style, a new Englishness in material form. Employing calico and chintzes in hangings, draperies and coverings, as well as Chinese porcelain or wallpaper, the prospects of Asia were recreated on a safely exotic stage, without the risks and inconvenience of foreign travel; the seraglio was hinted at, the delights of imagined gardens posed. These creations complemented the developing genteel aesthetic for the picturesque which shaped approved concepts of exterior vistas. Nature was being refined and representations of its vistas were in high demand, as long as they reflected the new aesthetic conventions.[34] Similarly, the alien sights of Asia could be framed in a sympathetic and comforting form in private interior sanctuaries, whether

Figure 1
The late-eighteenth-century figure termed "Coquette", seated in her boudoir, is framed by lush botanic designs in paper, cloth and furnishings that reinforce the sexuality implicit in her person. "The Coquette at her Toilet", Picture Library, Museum of London.

"closet," chamber or bedroom, with embellishments of painted garlands, trees-of-life, and lush bowers on fine cotton, or printed on paper, all redolent with natural images of fecundity. The late eighteenth-century figure termed "Coquette," seated in her boudoir, is framed in just this way by botanic designs in paper, cloth, and furnishings that reinforce the sexuality implicit in her person (see Figure 1). The symbolic meanings embedded in these motifs were sufficiently fluid to be acceptable to Western sensibilities and indeed are so familiar to modern eyes that they remain almost invisible unless we are prodded to look again. Contemporaries were far more sensitive to the images presented. In the early eighteenth century, the words Daniel Defoe used to describe what he saw as a disastrous economic trend conjures a covert and illicit intrusion: "It crept into our houses, our closets and bed-chambers; curtains, cushions, chairs and at last the beds themselves were nothing but Callicoes or Indian stuffs." Elizabeth Pepys was among those infected with the calico fancy, a fact recounted in her husband's diary notation of a shopping trip where, "after many tryalls bought my wife a Chinke [chintz]; that is, a paynted Indian Callico for to line her new Study, which is very pretty."[35]

Domestic space was not all by definition a private or secluded setting. Social events and even public occasions took place in various parts of the home. However, attitudes towards the spaces within the house changed over time. The bedroom, in particular, was becoming a private and intimate setting by the late seventeenth century, even among the broad middling classes. Within genteel circles, as the great rebuilding of England took place, houses now included hallways from which rooms could be accessed, with space put aside for bedrooms, designated private spaces for sleep, sexual encounters, procreation and the care of infants or the aged. The faces and forms of men and women were also recreated in these private spots; thus, our glance at "The Coquette at her Toilet" has a voyeuristic tone, recognizing the privacy invaded by our gaze. Those affluent enough to have an area allocated for beds and beddings fashioned these rooms to enhance privacy and comfort, with window curtains, bed curtains, quilts, carpets, and cushions.[36] This was the first domestic space to be conquered by calicos.

Lorna Weatherill's exhaustive study of consumer behavior does not focus specifically on bed furnishings. However, she did record the ownership of window curtains in her probate sample. Interestingly, the highest percentage of window curtains was found among tradesmen of various levels of affluence, followed by the gentry (see Figure 2). This in itself emphasizes the differing levels of importance given to novel commodities by consumers with different priorities and sensibilities. As Weatherill notes, the social hierarchy was not identical to the consumer hierarchy; income, opportunity and the significance ascribed to various commodities determined to a great degree their levels of consumption.[37] A letter from 1669 reported that "they are

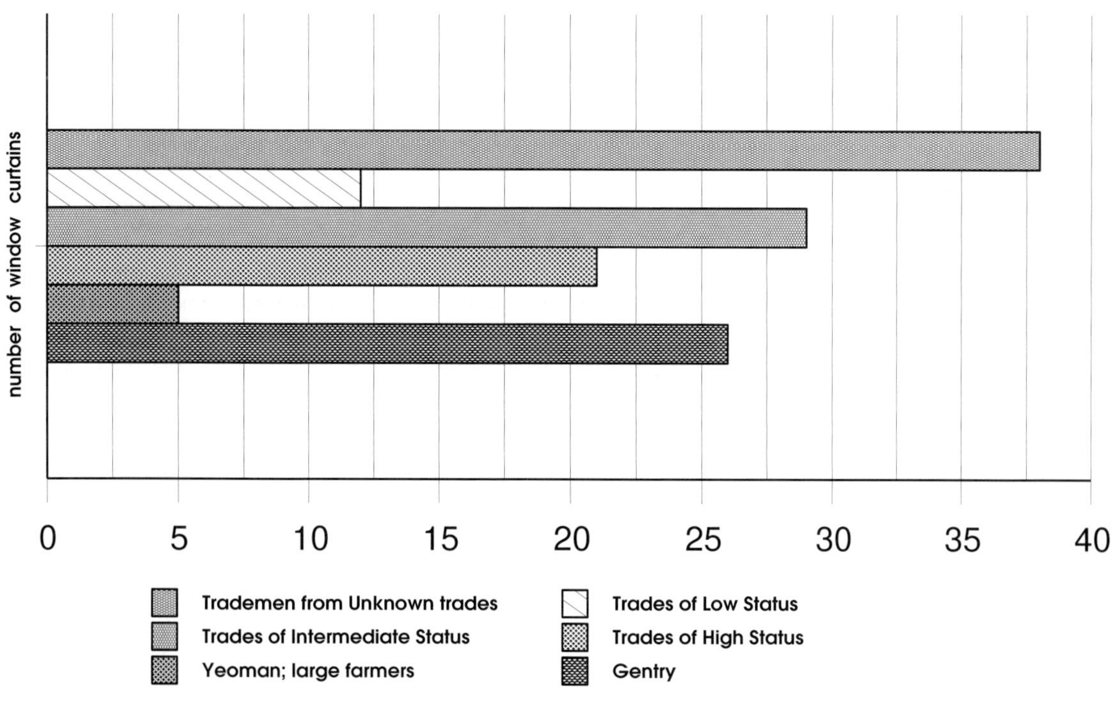

Source: Weatherill, p. 168, Table 8.1.

Figure 2
Ownership of Window Curtains in English Probate Inventory Sample, 1675–1725.

here in England . . . a great practice of printing large branches for hanging in [rooms] . . . and we do believe that . . . our Callicoes printed after that manner might vent well, and . . . we would have you send us 20,000 pieces. . ."[38] The evidence of the painted hangings, in combination with these facts, points to the breadth of the market for domestic soft furnishings in Indian floral styles. And, not content with the genteel market alone, East India Company directors urged that cheaper bed furnishings be "Ready made up of Several Sorts and Prices, strong, but none too dear, nor any overmean in regard you know our Poorest people in England lye without any Curtains or Vallances and our richest in Damask." The author hoped that "some of these things may gain that repute here as may give us cause of greater enlargement."[39] Their hopes were answered.

For Elizabeth Pepy's study, Queen Mary's private bedroom in Hampton Court, and the south London merchant Peter Proby's bedroom and "Closett"[40] chintz represented informality, languor, and indulgence; the intimacy and sensuality associated with these private spaces was intensified through the furnishings selected. Scrutiny of probate inventories reveals the decorative styles created by southern England's tradesmen and their wives. Proby's "Closett" boasted "Callicoe hangings about the Roome;"[41] a turn-of-the-century tobacco dealer in Oxford included a "callicoe bed" among his furnishings; a Blackfriar tailor created a best bedroom equipped with comfortable bed furnishings including "two Callicoe Curtaines one redd." The Essex house of a City Merchant Tailor boasted "Callicoe Curtains with double vallence and a Counterpain lined with dymity" in the white chamber, plus "Two Callicoe Curtains with som [*sic*] redd hangings" in the best bedroom. A haberdasher of modest resources displayed five calico window curtains in the main bedroom and Mrs. Jones, owner of a small chandler shop, draped a flowered calico quilt over one of her beds. The draperies found in the principal bedroom of a St. Giles haberdasher included "One Bedstead and Camblett furniture lined with callicoe."[42]

These refashioned domestic settings were peopled by characters keen to play their role as consumers, but also as players within new exoticized sites, sporting new costumes. Asian-inspired dress, modified and revised, held a particular fascination for men from the middling to elite ranks, who were especially beguiled by the decorative banyans or dressing gowns made of printed and painted silks and cottons. They chose to wear these loose flowered robes as they socialized with their most intimate friends and family, sometimes shod in curling "Turkish" slippers. The sweeping unstructured banyans were ideal mediums for display of full flowering patterns and the gowns remained favorites with men for the next several centuries. These garments represented a distinct change from "stiff Collar, bands and Cloake," as John Evelyn described his regular everyday clothing, conjuring up Asian-style luxury and ease. Samuel Pepys commented in his diary about the loose gown and turban worn by Sir Philip Howard when he called upon him at home—Pepys ensured that he was memorialized in his portrait painted in 1666, wearing a similar gown, which he rented since he did not yet have his own.[43] In Thomas Cole's shop, in 1667, amidst the rich array of East Indian and European textiles, were thirty-eight "Indian Gowns, small & great," with an average price of 5 shillings and 8 pence. Cole also sold other articles to enhance interior spaces, including looking glasses through which one's person and perspective could be admired.[44] I can image Pepys posturing in his borrowed banyan before a mirror, struggling to achieve the best pose for his portrait. Banyans continued to be readily available from specialist shops like that of the "Indian Gown Maker," Edward Gunn, who sold a profusion of plain and fancy robes for men as well as for women in Restoration London. His stock included gowns for men of "hand colloured Indian sattin . . . flowered grogram . . . small redd Indian sattin . . . [and] thirty ordinary gownes."[45] His competitor, John Broadhurst, offered men's morning gowns at a cost of £1 each for the growing numbers of men who sought to redefine the personal costume in which they spent their informal leisure hours.[46] It is not surprising that, in 1700, a flourishing mercer left a full range of bedroom furnishings in his estate—"green flowoure silk and quilt case curtains . . . two Callico quilts" plus "a Gown" for his personal use.[47] The taste for banyans continued undiminished and was met through specialist and general suppliers, with a continuing juxtaposition of seduction, informality, and intimacy with exotic botanic designs.[48] The early eighteenth-century banyan illustrated here (Figure 3) is a sumptuous example of a painted chintz garment containing Japanese design influences in the flowering tree, which covers the back and front of the garment. Imagine the

Figure 3
The early eighteenth-century banyan is a sumptuous example of a painted chintz garment containing Japanese design influences in the flowering tree, which covers the back and front of the garment. Imagine the gentleman, merchant or wealthy scion of a noble family swathed in this garment and we can readily see how men could be seduced by this style. 959.112, Royal Ontario Museum, Toronto.

gentleman, merchant or wealthy scion of nobility swathed in this garment and we can see how readily men were seduced by this style. In this way domestic privacy and intimacy were redefined within the gentry and middle ranks, as imaginative "Asian" landscapes were constructed in the home and Asian-style costumes worn as well.[49] Although some traditional cultural, gender, and economic interests were offended by the spread of Indian muslins, calicos, and chintzes, by the restyling of bedrooms and wardrobes, the diffusion of floral fabrics found supporters of both sexes.

Imitation and Invention

It is well known that, in 1721, the powerful woolen interests in England succeeded in having Parliament ban cottons, at least for a time. But theirs was a relative victory. Since the time that calicos were introduced in northern Europe, a process of cultural exchange had been put in play. Early on, European designers had instructed Indian crafts people in the colors and motifs most pleasing to Western eyes.[50] As we have seen, from there it was just a short step to imitating the Indian style in Europe itself—the Queen Anne era silk taffeta apron shown here depicts the enthusiastic floral adaptations of an English embroiderer (see Figure 4). Opportunities for printers were also evident and before the close of the seventeenth century, printing works were well established. In Marseille, Amsterdam and London the exotic was being domesticated, alien forms were given a more familiar look without losing their appeal and new generations continued to be enthralled by new-style botanic prints.[51]

Imitation followed in tandem with innovation, as painters, printers and weavers strived to replicate the banned Asian textiles, devising locally made facsimiles.[52] Counterfeits of Indian goods abounded, supplied in the next instance by European linen manufacturers and the British linen and cotton/linen industries. Over the eighteenth century the British cotton industry devised new production techniques that enabled them to make better copies of East Indian products. The variety, price and inventive printed designs, characteristic of East Indian textiles, were the models to which these manufacturers aspired. Ultimately, Indian textiles became naturalized.[53] This term is particularly apt in describing the chronological process of accommodation that took place. The *Oxford English Dictionary* defines "naturalize" as the process of assuming a new citizenship; it also refers to the vegetative process, the rooting and spreading of new flora in a once alien soil. In the hands of European artisans, printed fabrics

Figure 4
The early eighteenth-century era silk taffeta apron shown here shows the enthusiastic floral adaptations of an English embroiderer. 920.36.2, Royal Ontario Museum, Toronto.

Figure 5 and 6
The gown and petticoat illustrated here show mid-century garments, the former featuring tulips, carnations, and other botanic exotica created by Indian artisans and, if worn in England, worn illegally. The petticoat embroidery arises from a similar aesthetic, but was of English make. In sum, they created a figure at the apex of informal English fashion. 967.176.1 and 932.23 (detail), Royal Ontario Museum, Toronto.

(as well as embroideries) retained their botanic idiom, but gradually took on an indigenous Western character. By the mid-eighteenth century, the content of the scenic prints and the standardization of production transformed printed wares. The content and style of printed textiles evolved, as these goods became the new staples in domestic furnishings and personal wardrobes (see Figures 5 and 6). The gown and petticoat illustrated here show mid-century garments, the former featuring tulips, carnations, and other botanic exotica created by Indian artisans and, if worn in England, worn illegally. The petticoat embroidery arises from a similar aesthetic, but was of English make. In sum, they created a figure at the apex of informal English fashion.

My earlier qualitative study of consumption patterns indicated who bought and owed the new cotton consumer goods. I found a pattern of ever-widening ownership of cotton products among laboring women and working men, artisans and maid servants, home owners and shopkeepers, gentry and aspiring gentry. Collectively, these individuals bought, owned and used a growing assortment of cottons, from the 1730s to 1800s. My more recent quantitative sampling of pawned goods, owned by laboring and middling people, confirmed the broadening market for the cottons rolling out of warehouses in Manchester and Glasgow. Income, social standing, occupation, and, to a degree, geography, impinged on the capacity of men and women to purchase new consumer goods.[54] However, interest and demand

showed a surprising conformity. Even among the laboring classes, the market for flowered and patterned cottons extended into all but the poorest households. Over the eighteenth century there was a steady replacement of various wools, silks, linens and leathers with assorted cotton materials, many of which were dyed and printed in the latest flowered form in Britain (see, for example, Figure 7). By the 1770s, this transformation in dress and furnishings was a source of pride within British legislative circles and the naturalization process was complete as bolts of printed floral fabric came to epitomize the strength of industrial Britain. British trade in India was followed by formal imperial expansion over the eighteenth century, marking a new stage in relations with Asia. However, Englishness, indeed Britishness, was by this time stylistically defined by fabrics and motifs of Asian origin that had been absorbed into the patterns of daily life and reiterated in new forms over the years that followed. Simultaneously, fascination with the imagined landscapes of Asia created a widely shared cultural forum within England, which in turn contributed to what has been called the imagined community of England. In this way, the shared material and cultural botanic forms in dress, decor and landscape became parts of the idiom of everyday life.

Conclusion

Chintzes arrived at the same time as Europeans reconceived the natural world. And, as cities grew, there was less direct contact with the

Figure 7
This dress fragment is a British woodblock print on cotton fabric dating from about 1770 and shows a carnation-like flower twining across the fabric surface, very much in the Indian manner. 934.4.203, Royal Ontario Museum, Toronto.

exigencies of rural life.[55] In these circumstances the countryside became both "more accessible and yet more distant," as Brewer notes. However, "[i]t could be tamed and controlled by the technologies of taste."[56] Arriving at the time of an evolving aesthetic of nature, printed and painted East Indian textiles became a highly charged commodity through which the imagined vistas of an Asian Arcadia became part of the material of homely life. Asian manufactures gradually redefined expressions of privacy, of intimate relaxation, with flowered bedrooms and flowing banyans. Over time, these textile exotics became comfortable staples of respectable gentility, just as the tulip went from being a Turkish rarity to a Dutch trope. Calicos were naturalized over the eighteenth century and they became English. However, even in these forms the revised floral motifs were not static commodities.

A postscript in the calico trade arises from the re-export trade in East Indian textiles to the northern reaches of the North American continent. Over the eighteenth century, British imperial interests extended from the heart of the Indian subcontinent to the rivers and forests of the northern latitudes of America. North American aboriginal peoples had acquired calicos from Europeans since the seventeenth century;[57] the botanic depictions on painted and printed calicos resonated with First Nations' peoples and were among their preferred "Western" trade goods. Indeed, an early nineteenth-century diarist recounted the keen interest an Ojibwa woman took in her husband's flowered cotton dressing gown.[58] At the same time, Christian missionaries encouraged the substitution of these fashionable floral motifs for indigenous patterns in embroidered bead work, seeing this as a step towards a "civilized"

Western status. However, as Ruth Phillips aptly notes, "multivalency . . . rendered floral motifs mutually appropriable into Native and non-native contexts of artistry and use."[59] By the nineteenth century, floral designs were incorporated into beaded and embroidered items—caps, tea cozies, baskets, match holders, bookmarks, clothing, and the like—the work of eastern North America's aboriginal peoples. In many cases, surviving artifacts reveal designs with a visible debt to East Indian motifs. Thereafter, as Phillips shows, botanic-inspired patterns became a defining element of authentic aboriginal embroidered work and for generations thereafter the flowered output of north-eastern indigenous peoples was seen as a quintessential indigenous commodity. Vast quantities of beaded and other needleworks were sold to visiting Europeans and traveled to England, where the patterns were later reproduced as authentic Native American artistic designs and published for readers of Victorian needlework magazines. East Indian floral designs were transposed into Native American beaded goods then became another of the common decorative commodities in England's middle-class homes, another flowered ornament that fit so well with English decor. Thus, Asian and American cultures were linked through European intervention and a common fascination with floral idioms; Adam Smith's aphorism was made manifest through the calico trade.

The impact of East Indian textiles was profound in many ways and patterns of material life were transformed as a result. As English gardens assumed more complex forms with plants from Asia and the Americas, so new-style floral vistas were matched by similarly flowered household furnishings and dress; both came to epitomize the new English culture of the industrial age. Floral motifs were redefined and diffused, as calicos became a permanent feature of domestic furnishings and personal adornment, a symbol of genteel repose, of male informality, and intimacy, evolving to become a constant component of Western material culture and thereby refashioning the domestic world.

Acknowledgments

This project was supported by a research grant from the Social Sciences and Humanities Research Council of Canada. An earlier version of this article was presented at the conference East & West: Luxury and the Exotic, University of Warwick, 2000. I would like to thank the curators and staff at the Royal Ontario Museum, Toronto, for their generous and ongoing assistance.

Notes

1. Adam Smith, *An Inquiry into the Nature and Causes of the Wealth of Nations* (1776, reprinted 1981, Indianapolis IN: Liberty Press), vol. 2, p. 626.
2. Some of the recent works on this subject include Julia Ching and Willard Oxtoby (eds), *Discovering China: European Interpretations in the Enlightenment* (Rochester NY: University of Rochester Press, 1992); Ken Arnold, "Trade, Travel, and Treasure: Seventeenth-Century Artificial

Curiosities" in Chloe Chard and Helen Langdon (eds), *Transports: Travel, Pleasure, and Imaginative Geography, 1600–1830* (New Haven CT: Yale University Press, 1996); Prasannan Parthasarathi, "Rethinking Wages and Competitiveness in the Eighteenth Century: Britain and South India," *Past and Present* no. 158, 1998, pp. 79–109; David Porter, "Chinoiserie and the Aesthetics of Illegitimacy," *Studies in Eighteenth-Century Culture* 28, 1999, pp. 27–54; Kenneth Pomeranz, *The Great Divergence: China, Europe, and the Making of the Modern World Economy* (Princeton NJ: Princeton University Press, 2000); Maxine Berg, "From Imitation to Invention: Creating Commodities in Eighteenth-Century Britain," *Economic History Review* 55: 1, 2002, pp. 1–30.

3. There have been extensive studies of these cabinets of curiosities. See, for example, Anthony Alan Shelton, "Cabinets of Transgression: Renaissance Collections and the Incorporation of the New World" in John Elsner and Roger Cardinal (eds), *The Culture of Collecting* (Cambridge MA: Harvard University Press, 1994); Joy Kenseth, "A World of Wonders in One Closet Shut" in Joy Kenseth (ed.), *The Age of the Marvellous* (Chicago IL: University of Chicago Press, 1993); Arthur MacGregor, "The Cabinet of Curiosities in Seventeenth-Century Britain" in Oliver Impey and Arthur MacGregor (eds), *The Origins of Museums* (Oxford: Clarendon Press, 1985); Arthur MacGregor, *Tradescant's Rarities: Essays on the Foundation of the Ashmolean Museum* (Oxford: Clarendon Press, 1983).

4. Beverly Lemire, *Fashion's Favourite: The Cotton Trade and the Consumer in Britain, 1660–1800* (Oxford: Oxford University Press, 1991), pp. 23–9; Parthasarathi, "Rethinking Wages", pp. 79–82.

5. *Prince Butler's Tale: Representing the State of the Wool-Case, or the East-India Case Truly States* (London, 1699).

6. Otto Charles Thieme, *By Inch of Candle: A Sale at East-India-House*, 21 September 1675 (Minneapolis MN: The Associates of the James Ford Bell Library, University of Minnesota, 1982), Appendix, p. 23.

7. Lorna Weatherill, *Consumer Behaviour and Material Culture in Britain, 1660–1760* (London: Routledge, 1988), pp. 25–42.

8. Edward Roberts and Karen Parker, eds, *Southampton Probate Inventories, 1497–1575*, vol. I, (Southampton: Southampton University Press, 1992), p. xvii.

9. Roberts and Parker, *Southampton Probate Inventories*, vol. I, pp. 65–70; 150–2; 159–62; 165–7; vol. II, pp. 244–52; 346–7; 358–9.

10. M. F. S. Hervey, *Life of Thomas, Earl of Arundel*, p. 90, quoted in Joan Evans, *Patterns in Western Europe, 1180–1900*, vol. II (Oxford: Oxford University Press, 1931), p. 60; Therle Hughes, *English Domestic Needlework, 1660–1860* (London: Lutterworth Press, 1961), p. 34.

11. John Irwin and Katherine Brett, *Origins of Chintz, with a Catalogue of Indo-European Cotton-paintings in the Victoria and Albert Museum, London, and the Royal Ontario Museum, Toronto* (London: HMSO, 1970), pp. 1–4; K. N. Chaudhuri, *The Trading World of Asia and the English East India Company* (Cambridge: Cambridge University Press, 1978), p. 7.

12. This comprised 84% of the English trade with India at that time. Chaudhuri, *Trading World*, pp. 96–7, 282.

13. *Letter Book* IX, p. 106, quoted in P. J. Thomas, *Mercantilism and the East India Trade* (London: P. S. King & Son Ltd, 1926), p. 44.

14. Beverly Lemire, "Transforming Consumer Custom: Linen, Cotton and the English Market, 1660–1780" in Philip Ollerenshaw and Brenda Collins (eds), *Linen in Europe* (Oxford: Oxford University Press, 2003) in press.

15. Jack Goody, *The Culture of Flowers* (Cambridge: Cambridge University Press, 1993), pp. 2, 213.

16. Ruth B. Phillips, *Trading Identities: The Souvenir in Native North American Art from the Northeast, 1700–1900* (Montreal: McGill-Queens University Press, 1998), p. 158.

17. Goody, *Culture of Flowers*, p. 214.

18. Anna Pavord, *The Tulip* (London: Bloomsbury, 2002).

19. Simon Schama, *The Embarrassment of Riches: An Interpretation of Dutch Culture*

in the Golden Age (London: Collins, 1987), pp. 350–7.

20. Raleigh Trevelyan, *Shades of Alhambra* (1984), p. 7, quoted in Jane Brown, *The Pursuit of Paradise: A Social History of Gardens and Gardening* (London: HarperCollins, 1999), p. 23.

21. David Underdown, *Revel, Riot and Rebellion: Popular Politics and Culture in England, 1603–1660* (Oxford: Oxford University Press, 1985), pp. 96, 178, 261, 283; John Prest, *The Garden of Eden: The Botanic Garden and the Re-Creation of Paradise* (New Haven, CT: Yale University Press, 1981).

22. Goody, *Culture of Flowers*, pp. 214–20.

23. In William Temple, *Upon the Gardens of Epicurus, with other XVIIth Century Garden Essays* (London, 1908).

24. Brown, *Pursuit of Paradise*, pp. 27–42; Chandra Mukerji, "Reading and Writing with Nature: a Materialist Approach to French Formal Gardens" in J. Brewer and R. Porter (eds), *Consumption and the World of Goods* (London: Routledge, 1993), pp. 452–7. J. Evelyn, in J. Bowle (ed.), *The Diary of John Evelyn* (Oxford: Oxford University Press, 1985), pp. 47, 70–1, 241.

25. Sir Thomas Brown, *The Garden of Cyrus; Or, the Quincuncial Lozenge* . . . in Temple, *Gardens of Epicurus*, p. 153.

26. Goody, *Culture of Flowers*, p. 2; John Brewer, *The Pleasures of the Imagination: English Culture in the Eighteenth Century* (London: Fontana Press, 1997), p. 620.

27. See Elizabeth Kowaleski-Wallace, *Consuming Subjects: Women, Shopping, and Business in the Eighteenth Century* (New York: Columbia University Press, 1997) and especially pp. 52–72 for perspectives on the relationship between women consumers and china.

28. Roberts and Parker, *Southampton Probate Inventories*, p. xxv.

29. T215.1979; T5.1880; 75a 1880; Textile Collection, Victoria and Albert Museum, London.

30. Hughes, *English Domestic Needlework*, p. 34.

31. *Letter Book* 1641, quoted in G. P. Baker, *Calico Printing and Painting in the East Indies in the XVIIth and XVIIIth Centuries* (London: Edward Arnold, 1921), p. 30.

32. Hughes, *English Domestic Needlework*, p. 36.

33. Ibid.

34. Brewer, *Pleasures*, pp. 631–41.

35. Daniel Defoe, *Weekly Review* 31 January 1708; Robert Latham and William Matthews (eds), *The Diary of Samuel Pepys* (Berkeley CA: University of California Press, 1972), vol. IV, p. 299.

36. Weatherill, *Consumer Behaviour*, pp. 159–60. Vickery notes that in the eighteenth century only favored female guests were invited into the bedrooms of the eighteenth-century Lancashire genteel to see their hostess's new treasures. Amanda Vickery, *The Gentleman's Daughter: Women's Lives in Georgian England* (London: Yale University Press, 1998), p. 206.

37. Weatherill, *Consumer Behaviour*, pp. 168–85.

38. *Letter Book* 1669, quoted in J. Irwin and P. R. Schwartz, *Studies in Indo-European Textile History* (Ahmedabad: Calico Museum of Textile, 1966), p. 52.

39. *Letter Book* 1682, quoted in Irwin and Schwartz, *Indo-European Textile*, pp. 36–7.

40. Latham and Matthews (eds), *Diary of Samuel Pepys,* vol. IV, p. 299; Thomas, *Mercantilism*, p. 28; PROB 5 1892, Public Record Office, London.

41. PROB 5 1892, PRO.

42. PROB 5, 2268, 3731, 3790, 3961, PRO; Ms 9174/28, Guildhall Library, London; W P 25 May 1704, Oxfordshire Archives.

43. Evelyn, *Diary*, p. 216; Latham and Matthews (eds), *Diary of Samuel Pepys*, vol. VII, pp. 378, 602.

44. 301 Inventory, Court of Orphans, Corporation of London Record Office (CLRO).

45. AM/P1 (1) 1673/33, London Metropolitan Archives.

46. 2262 Inventory, Court of Orphans, CLRO.

47. PROB 5, 640, PRO.

48. The 1734 inventory of over 300 very diverse garments from a London-based clothes manufacturer included "Two Banyons," suggesting the ubiquity of these goods. PROB 3, 33/105, PRO.

49. Norbert Elias, *The Civilizing Process: The History of Manners*, trans. Edmund Jephcott (1939, Oxford: Blackwell, 1978), pp. 160–9; E. A. Entwistle, *A Literary History of Wallpaper* (London: Batsford, 1969); O. Impey, *Chinoiserie: The Impact of Oriental Styles on Western Art and Decoration* (New York: Oxford University Press, 1977); Anna Somers Cocks, "The Nonfunctional Use of Ceramics in the English Country House during the Eighteenth Century," *Studies in the History of Art* 25, 1998, pp. 195–215; John Crowley, *The Invention of Comfort: Sensibilities and Design in Early Modern Britain and Early America* (Baltimore MD: Johns Hopkins University Press, 2001).

50. Irwin and Schwartz, *Indo-European Textile*, pp. 17, 34, 52–3.

51. Simon Schama first employed the phrase "domesticated . . . exoticism." Schama, *Embarrassment of Riches*, p. 196.

52. Maxine Berg notes that: "much of the focus of invention during the eighteenth century was directed towards this process of imitation." Maxine Berg, "New Commodities, Luxuries and Their Consumers in Eighteenth-century England" in M. Berg and H. Clifford (eds), *Consumers and Luxury: Consumer Culture in Europe, 1650–1850* (Manchester: Manchester University Press, 1999), p. 77.

53. Lemire, *Fashion's Favourite*, pp. 33–4, 42, 77–85.

54. Lemire, *Fashion's Favourite*, Appendix 2, pp. 205–19; Beverly Lemire, "The Fashion for Cottons: Asian Trade, Domestic Industry and Consumer Demand in Eighteenth Century Europe" in David Jenkins (ed.), *The Cambridge History of Western Textiles* (Cambridge: Cambridge University Press, 2003) (in press). It is also worth noting that less affluent buyers employed various strategies to extend their options in the marketplace, such as the trade in secondhand goods.

55. Brewer, *Pleasures*, pp. 621–43.

56. Brewer, *Pleasures*, p. 641.

57. A 15/1, *Grand Journal*, 1676–81, Hudson's Bay Company, Hudson's Bay Company Archives, Winnipeg, Manitoba.

58. Phillips, *Trading Identifies*, p. 171.

59. Phillips, *Trading Identifies*, p. 157.

Exhibition Review
The Jerwood Applied Arts Prize Exhibition 2002: Textiles. Crafts Council Gallery, London
19 September–3 November 2002

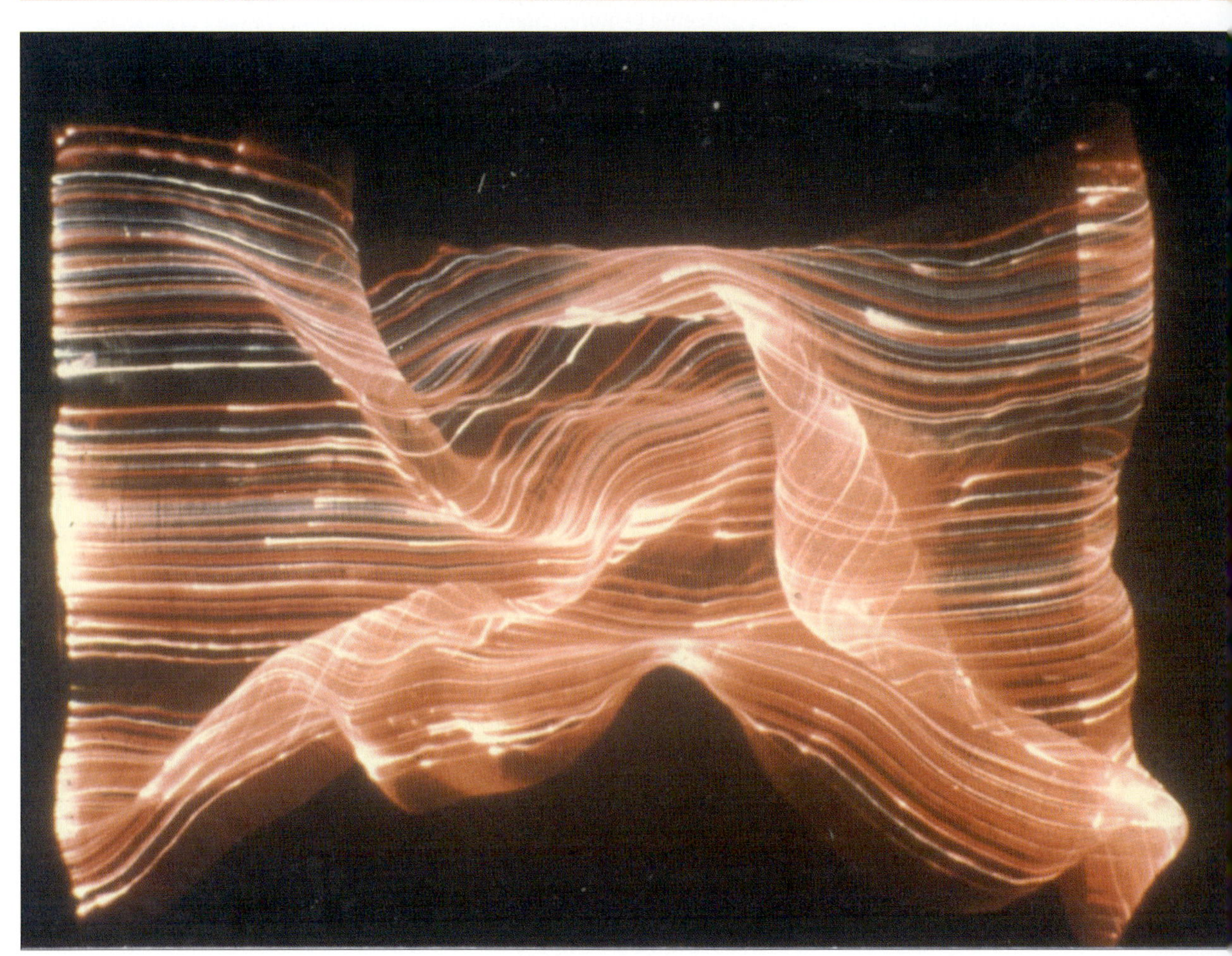

Exhibition Review
The Jerwood Applied Arts Prize Exhibition 2002: Textiles. Crafts Council Gallery, London 19 September–3 November 2002

The annual *Jerwood Applied Arts Prize Exhibition* opened in September 2002 at the Crafts Council Gallery in London. The £15,000 annual award runs on a five-yearly cycle: ceramics, textiles, glass, furniture, and jewelry. This categorization itself raises questions and concerns, opening itself up, as it does, to a mixture of materials and subject disciplines. In the context of the 2002 exhibition, the second time around for textiles, we might ask ourselves how a material can be adjudicated with rigor when, as a subject discipline, textiles is so diverse. In Britain the established structures of higher education, which support the subject area, are broadly based; out of them develops professional engagement that flows across the full breadth of contemporary visual art and design practice.

The short-list for this second round reveals that the judges have struggled precisely with these problems of diversity, which is not to decry their expertise,[1] but rather the problems associated with the task in hand. The diversity within the category of ceramics poses similar concerns, and both subject areas would benefit from the opportunity to debate such matters prior to the third round of the Jerwood, if the award is to continue to attract prestige.

An exhibition formed out of an open selection does not readily create coherent viewing, but a light curatorial hand has produced some thought-provoking juxtapositions, allowing for critical considerations which move beyond material, tradition, and skill. In the front gallery was work by Shizuko Kimura, Clio Padovani, Shelly Goldsmith, and Freddie Robins. A pair of Kimura's "hand-stitched" life drawings was displayed, stretched inside and constricted by a traditional frame. This can be read as a challenge to the historic conformities of fine art. Where Kimura's "embroideries" were

REVIEWED BY POLLY BINNS

Textile, Volume 1, Issue 1, pp. 87–91
Reprints available directly from the Publishers.
Photocopying permitted by licence only.

allowed to hang free, in three large sections through and around which the viewer could walk, the transparency of the cotton muslin defied any logic of a front and reverse to the images. Stitch and loose thread became pure mark-making and a drawing mastery of the hand/eye relationship, an ageless and timeless "human" technology.

Kimura's framed pieces could be seen in relation to *Close* (2001), an installation by Clio Padovani, in which a light-box construction explored, through imagery and technology, the relationship between traditional tapestry weave and the pixel of the computer "brain." The manner of presentation challenged our perceptions of woven and digital processes and their shifting location within contemporary visual art practice.

Shelly Goldsmith chose to install *Further Ruminations on the Pear Shaped Organ* (2002) on a stark and industrial stainless-steel trolley. This isolated and made unbearably vulnerable the tapestry-woven "organs," each with the warp threads left dangling. Associations with the umbilical cord sprang to mind, or of hopes raised by the donor transplant organ. The tenuous thread of life in this age of medical intervention was further echoed in the center of the gallery where, raised on a transparent perspex plinth, lay *Skin—A Good Thing To Live In* (2002), by Freddie Robins: a life-size, pale pink, knitted human form, flattened and empty. Robins implied an element of humor in the title, and also in the crossed-over finger on a boned-out hand, a universal sign of hope. However, "cloth as skin" takes on multiple cultural resonances, from the flayed figure of mythological fable to contemporary society's obsession with the nip and tuck of the plastic surgeon. We were denied a view of the underside/inside of the "other."

The work of Maxine Bristow quietly and authoritatively dominated the second gallery. The

Figure 1
Shelly Goldsmith. *Ruminations on a Pear Shaped Organ* (2002).

installation of her 2002 piece, *18 × 51 over 11.44*, along the full length of a naturally lit wall invited the viewer to move along its length in intimate relationship to its surface. However, when the viewer stood back, the implicit architectural qualities took precedence. These monumental "bag" series have been widely exhibited in the international arena and articulate her continuing interest in a minimalist aesthetic. Bristow also presented a body of emerging work, which evinced an interest in the familiarity of those elements within the interior that have an "invisibility" in playing a supporting role to a building's main architectural features. Her cloth "banister" and "railing" installations are produced by means of an obsessive needlepoint process that she has developed with the support of a group of embroidery amateurs, those makers whose traditional outlets have been the liturgical kneeler or the domestic needlepoint picture "kit." Juxtaposed to Bristow's work in this

Figure 2
Shizuko Kimura. *Caribbean* (2000).

Sarah Taylor. *Fibre Optic Form. (Red, blue & white phase)* (1997).

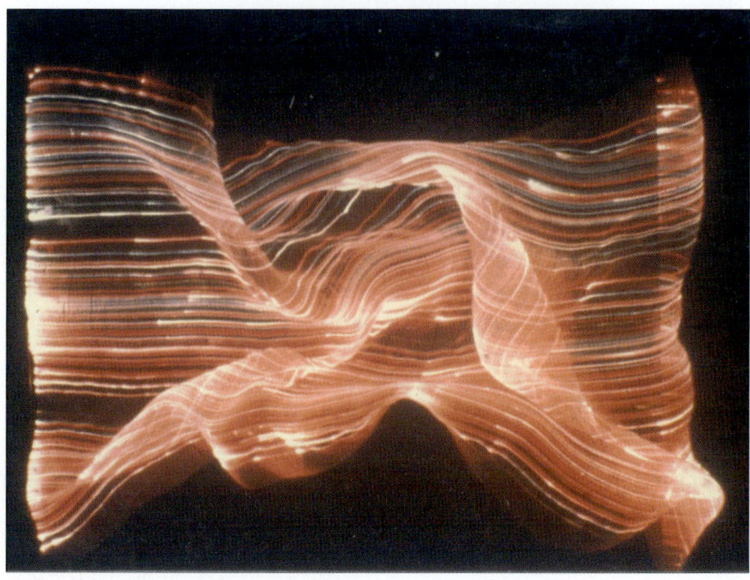

gallery were the monumental "appliqué" landscapes of Rowena Dring, which echo the pop-art ethos of the billboard advert or the comic strip. They similarly evoked canvas needlepoint "kits," where the painted landscape image presented for the maker's instruction celebrates romantic and heritage traditions.

Sarah Taylor's fiber optics were wall-based works of light and illusion that sought to redefine the surrounding space—"the area between the work and its audience is by no means a neutral or an independent entity," comments the catalog essay by Lesley Millar (p. 4). Unfortunately, the rather clumsily contained space in the gallery did little to realize the potential of the work. Displayed in the center of the gallery Lauren Moriarty's pierced rubber lengths and cube constructions revealed both their intimate complexity and their potential for filtering light and

shadow. What was less clear was their location within avant-garde textile practice. This was the work of a very new maker, which has not yet developed a clear identity and it was seen to disadvantage in this context.

Problematic overall was the intrusive exhibition design, which gave off inappropriate messages. The exhibition text and statements made by each artist were presented on lengths of drab brown, industrially produced felt, which reminded one uncomfortably of approaches to fiber work in the 1970s. The text itself was manufactured by industrial embroidery processes redolent of the cheap end of high-street fashion, whilst the artist statements were headed by a facsimile of each one's signature, associative of "yuppie culture" obsession with designer labels. The lengths divided up the gallery space and introduced constraints into the viewing of the work, all of which was diminished by the intrusion. This design approach represented a worrying misreading of the work by the Crafts Council.

Particularly welcome, for the long-term evaluation of the exhibition, is the illustrated catalog, which includes a thoughtful and sensitive essay in response to the work by Lesley Millar. She describes it as "a verbal gallery constructed by the writer, to house the work, or a placing of elements in order—a 'tidying of a room'" (Millar 2002: 4). This proves a successful approach for negotiating the diversity of the work and the declared ambitions of each maker. The lack of the artists' own statements in the catalog seems an inexplicable omission.

The exhibition goes on national tour to Salford, Kilkenny, and Belfast until July 2003. The announcement of the winner of the 2002 Jerwood Applied Arts Award in Textiles was made on 30 September 2002, after the submission date for this review. To find out details of the winner go on to the Crafts Council website—www.craftscouncil.org.uk

Note

1. The selection panel was made up of Caroline Broadhead, textile artist and winner of the Jerwood Applied Arts Prize: Textiles in 1997; Nina Campbell, interior designer; Pamela Johnson (Chair), independent writer, critic, and curator; Linda Parry, Deputy Keeper of Furniture, Textiles and Fashion at the Victoria and Albert Museum, London, and Yinka Shonibare, artist.

References

Millar, Lesley. 2002. Catalogue essay, *Jerwood Applied Arts Prize 2002: Textiles*. London: Crafts Council.

Exhibition Review

Trading Places: The East India Company and Asia 1600–1834. The British Library, London
24 May–22 September 2002

Exhibition Review
Trading Places: The East India Company and Asia 1600–1834.
The British Library, London
24 May–22 September 2002

The British Library is the prime holder of the surviving archives of the East India Company. From its inception in 1600 the company quickly grew to become effectively one of the first multinational companies, controlling trade over half of the world. Over four hundred years of managing international trade from a great distance resulted in an extensive documentary legacy. For the most part this is mainly evidence from the London headquarters in the form of order books, correspondence, regulations, and a large amount of detail concerning the lives of the company's servants, etc. Now a part of the Oriental and India Office Collection, the archives provide the starting point for *Trading Places: The East India Company and Asia 1600–1834*. The exhibition is principally an exercise in the use of primary evidence and therefore offers valuable information rather than insight or analysis.

Although some of this material emanates from the trading posts and has an Asian perspective, it is mainly derived from a Eurocentric viewpoint; the product of Western eyes and minds. It is, therefore, rightly presented as the history of a company that traded with Asia, rather than a history of East–West trade. This might be a problem for some—who may interpret it as an abdication of responsibility and who may want to ask more searching questions about whose history it really is. In the process we are, however, made aware of the importance of the cultural exchange between Asia and Europe and the continuing influence of Asian culture on British life today, in particular the lasting legacy we owe to the impact of Indian textiles.

Undoubtedly there are complex issues involved in effective exhibition display and interpretation; particularly with more emotive subjects there is a need to unravel myth from fact. In true library tradition this display is dense with facts. Nevertheless, the selection of material and the chosen methods of display can clearly skew an evidence-based exhibition any

Textile, Volume 1, Issue 1, pp. 93–97
Reprints available directly from the Publishers.
Photocopying permitted by licence only.
© 2003 Berg. Printed in the United Kingdom.

way a curator wishes to take it. The data and the material evidence may be presented here in a seemingly disinterested manner, but one cannot help but wonder about the mass of evidence available and question why this item or that was chosen. The visual result has a rather static quality; an atmosphere of controlled intensity and quiet contemplation is created, eminently suitable for the library venue. The densely written text panels and labels require close attention from the visitor and are backed up with yet more information in the form of audio guides, leaflets and a substantial book.

As its title suggests this exhibition has two major themes—trade and the places most directly affected by that trade. The twin

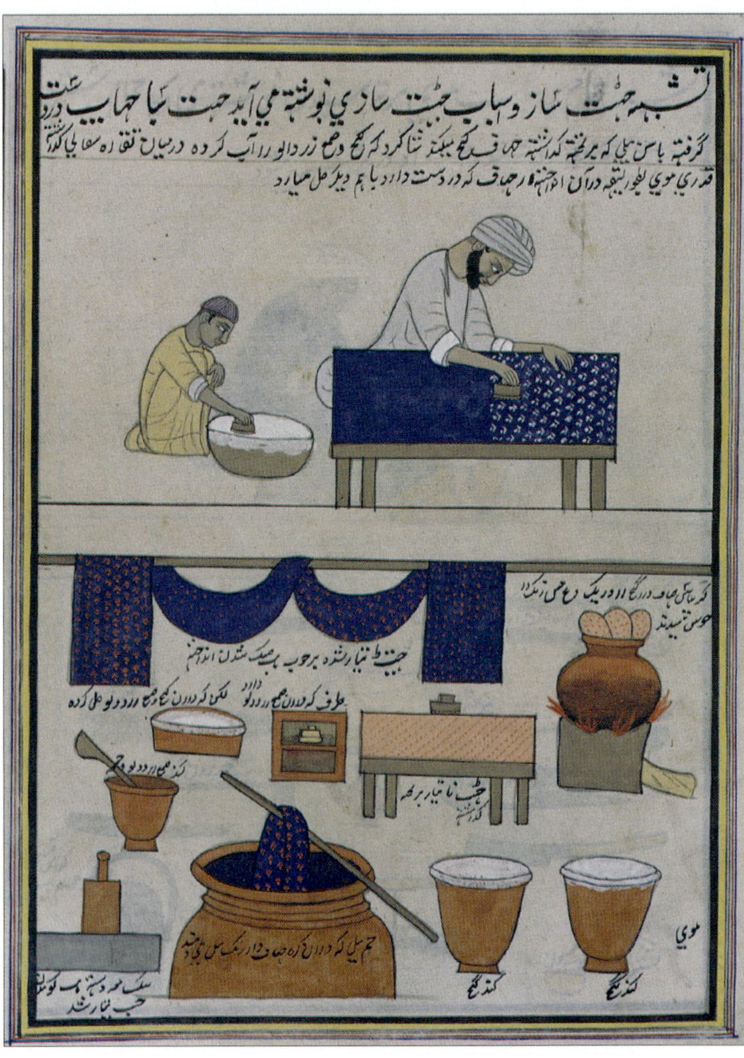

Figure 1

A cloth printer using a hand-block and a dyer, by a Kashmiri artist, *c.* 1850–60 (British Library, OIOC: Add.Or. 1714).

themes seek to present a comprehensive history of the large-scale narrative of East and West enterprise. The curator, Anthony Farrington, until recently head of the India Office Records at the British Library, chronicles the gains and losses experienced on both sides. The exhibition maps back and forth between the logistics of trade with its perilous journeys, the objects of trade (their economic rather than aesthetic values), and those places and people most directly affected by the production or consumption of the trade goods.

International trade was already well established when Britain started trading with Asia, and Indian textiles were being traded as far as South-East Asia, Persia, and the Red Sea ports. As this exhibition makes clear, the East India Company officials needed the cooperation and partnership of Asian traders in order to negotiate the intricate local markets and place their orders. It was certainly not all working against the interests of those already involved in the Indian Ocean trade, who retained tight control over sophisticated and buoyant internal and external markets. Asian merchants saw the economic benefits of extending their trade into Europe and

Figure 2

A cloth merchant seated in his shop, selling chintz to a customer, by a Tanjore artist, *c.* 1800 (British Library, OIOC: Add.Or. 2531).

granted trading rights to British merchants.

Cloth became the main item of the company's trade, quickly supplanting spices, the initial reason for trading in Asia. The variety of textiles from India alone was huge; a definitive glossary of textile types has yet to be compiled. As early as 1620, 50,000 pieces of printed and "pencilled" chintz were purchased for English consumption. One exhibited document listed Bengal piece goods destined for the London 1730–1 season; it describes 38 types of cloth, divided into 98 varieties. Indian textiles accounted for 60% of the total value of the company's sales in London as late as the 1750s.

Although documents are the starting point, informing both the interpretive materials and accompanying book, and are a wonderful resource for researchers, they do not always make for riveting exhibitions. The curator has wisely selected a variety of items from the vast company archive and the result is a diverse range of 200 items on display. They offer us material evidence in the form of paintings, prints, drawings, shipwreck materials, and small textile samples from order books. Some of the more prominent items, however, are the surviving objects of the textile and ceramic trades, borrowed from other institutions.

The Victoria and Albert Museum in London loaned some extraordinary textiles to augment the British Library holdings. They are mainly eighteenth-century examples of Indian exports and are large-scale, spectacular examples of printed and embroidered cottons and silks. For the most part they are luxury items, produced in the Indian subcontinent specifically for the European market and, as such, made fortunes for the Indian and British merchants who traded in them. These, then, were objects of admiration not appropriation, demanded by consumers who clearly wanted a wider choice than that previously available. Although not representative of the piece goods that formed the bulk of India's textile exports, they clearly show why Indian textiles soon supplanted the important spice trade and became the major items in the company order books. They give a sense of the extraordinary high standards achieved by Indian artisans, evident in the wide range of designs, sense of color, weaving, dyeing, printing, "pencilling," and embroidery skills on display.

For the newcomer to this trading history this exhibition is a good place to start. Those looking for debate about the history of relations between East and West will be disappointed; it does not question too closely the moral consequences of the global market. Nor does it acknowledge the growing proliferation of colonial studies, or studies in imperialism and orientalism over the past half-century. A series of lectures, which supports the exhibition, does, however, address the more controversial aspects of East–West trade links.

Exhibition Review

Of Gardens and Castles. Naturalistic Silks from the Eighteenth Century. Abegg-Stiftung, Riggisberg, near Berne, Switzerland
28 April–10 November 2002

Exhibition Review
Of Gardens and Castles. Naturalistic Silks from the Eighteenth Century.
Abegg-Stiftung, Riggisberg, near Berne, Switzerland
28 April–10 November 2002

The sensory experience of an exhibition at the Abegg-Stiftung begins well before you enter the unpretentious 1960s building that houses the magnificent private collection of textiles and works of art, originally put together by the Swiss textile industrialist and collector Werner Abegg and his American wife Margaret. In order to reach the darkened galleries in which the foundation's annual exhibition is housed, visitors have to pass through the verdant, picturesque landscape of the canton of Berne. Seemingly remote from the nearest village, the museum nestles amid imposing mountains, dotted with "chocolate-box" chalets with luxuriant, geranium-laden window boxes, the tranquillity of the setting broken only by the rhythmic jangle of cow bells. This immersion in the countryside, both its raw and domesticated forms, felt a particularly appropriate prelude to the mid-eighteenth-century "naturalistic" silks that glowed this year in the temporary exhibition space. The silks, dating from about 1730 to 1750, are virtuoso confections in which the natural and the man-made, the exuberant and the urbane, jostle companionably for attention in the composition of their designs. *Of Gardens and Castles. Naturalistic Silks from the Eighteenth Century* represented well the aesthetic and technical diversity of what were, in their time, the most elaborate and costly patterned silks manufactured in Europe and worn at princely courts. Some sixty woven silks were on show, just under one-third of those that the foundation owns and that are described in detail in the catalog raisonné published to coincide with the exhibition (Jolly 2002).

The Abegg-Stiftung is well known to many students of textiles

REVIEWED BY LESLEY ELLIS MILLER

Textile, Volume 1, Issue 1, pp. 99–105
Reprints available directly from the Publishers.
Photocopying permitted by licence only.

because of the wealth of its textile holdings, its educational mission in textile conservation, and its research publications. The collection has long had well-defined geographic and chronological boundaries: objects originated in Europe, the Mediterranean and the region of the silk routes and they date from antiquity to about 1800. Other facets of past collecting policy are more elusive. It seems, however, that the aesthetic appeal of the pieces (their intricate patterns), rather than their technical qualities or the historical context of their production and consumption, drove the Abeggs' original endeavors. They acquired most items through art dealers in Europe (especially Italy) and the U.S. from the 1930s onwards and usually, even after considerable research, only a partial provenance is available (Jolly 2002: 365). Not surprisingly, many of the mid-eighteenth-century woven silks have siblings in other museums in other parts of the world, often supplied by the same art dealers (e.g. Cat. no. 158). Cocooned in acid-free tissue paper in museum stores, few have been published in black and white, let alone color. Examples do appear periodically in exhibitions and publications devoted to much broader time spans or themes, exhibitions that are the antithesis of the regular, tightly focused displays that are a salient feature of the Abegg's activities and the springboard for conferences and allied publications around specific historical issues. In the recent past, aficionados have reveled in floral-patterned eighteenth-century English silks (Rothstein 1998), and in "bizarre" silks, those strange European textiles dating from the 1680s to the 1720s that owed so much to Oriental design sources (Ackermann 2000).

Of Gardens and Castles adopted a similarly specialist and scholarly approach. Basing itself on the stylistic chronology pioneered by Peter Thornton (1965), it engaged with variations within just one of his stylistic labels, and thus revealed the nuances of the style and its development from fairly two-dimensional depictions of variegated vegetation to full-blown and recognizable flowers, fruit, shells, etc. that can almost be picked off the fabric. The introduction of the use of *points rentrés* in the early 1730s changed the complexion of this kind of woven design, as different colors of weft threads interlocked to produce subtle tonal differences, creating, for example, convincingly velvety pomegranates and prickly pineapples (Cat. nos 126 and 127). This focus on one style also highlighted the fact that these silks were not unique one-off pieces but rather belonged to families of products manufactured in different colorways, sometimes with motifs that were mixed and matched or reversed to give different effects (Cat. nos 147 a, b). Clever visual comparisons and juxtapositions alluded to the realities of commercial production, the use of minor variations on a theme in order to create novelties. The sheer quantity and variety of similar patterns shattered the illusion that the few images that are so familiar from existing publications, and far too often attributed to the Lyonnais designer Jean Revel (1684–1751), were the only designs within this genre at a time when the silk industry of Lyons alone boasted over 2,000 master weavers and sixty freelance designers active in the making and designing of such silks (AML 1758). Moreover, while the Lyonnais were at the forefront in silk manufacture, they had many competitors and copyists in different parts of Europe (Poni 1997; Thornton 1965). Admittedly, it took weavers a long time to produce such complex silks on their manually operated drawlooms, but even so, they were making a much wider variety of goods than existing decorative arts literature often suggests. This exhibition proved that point.

It is truly remarkable that a single textile collection can offer this insight into eighteenth-century production through a selection from its own holdings of silks. The Abegg-Stiftung does not supplement its exhibitions with loans from elsewhere, nor, in turn, does it lend to other institutions, so visitors are likely to find something new to whet their appetites whatever the theme of the year. This institutional context—the pattern of collecting and the range and nature of the pieces—has serious implications for every exhibition, just as the physical environment does. Visitors must progress

Figure 1
Eighteenth-Century Silk. Reproduced with permission of The Abegg-Stiftung. Photographer: Christoph von Virag.

through the permanent displays in order to reach the two rooms that are available for temporary exhibitions, one of which is suitable for extremely large pieces of fabric. Both are lined with austere anthracite gray wallcoverings, the fiber-optic lighting is discreet, and the atmosphere suitably reverential. Silence reigned. The displays were comfortingly traditional, fresh, clean, and accessible (the classic black cube effect): in both rooms, flat textile panels dominated the space, hung on the walls behind non-reflective glass, veritable paintings without frames. Background and lighting enhanced the textural qualities of the silks, drew out the great variety of yarns (fancy and plain, gold and silver) and woven construction (velvet, gold and silver tissue, satin, taffeta, twill) and encouraged close inspection of motifs as well as long distance wonder at the complexity of the compositions and how designs worked in repeat once two or more widths were joined. This hang seemed perfectly apposite, as

Figure 2

Eighteenth-Century Silk. Reproduced with permission of The Abegg-Stiftung. Photographer: Christoph von Virag.

many of the silks would have been used as wall hangings in the eighteenth century. Indeed, the presence of some double and quadruple panels (Cat. no. 166), sometimes with their original gold passementerie edgings, was exciting as so few of the seamed panels originally inset into the paneling in the interiors of private (aristocratic) mansions have survived the depredations of heirs or dealers anxious to recycle fabrics for other household or dress purposes, or to maximize their financial assets by melting down the silks for their gold and silver content or by separating them into widths that could be sold individually. Of course, many of the panels showed the signs of recycling, often into or out of ecclesiastical ornaments of one sort or another (Cat. no. 147a).

The second room recognized that naturalism was not unique to textile design. Through a very simple *mise-en-scène*, the curator and designer conjured up an impression of the different uses of silks, and how their motifs found parallels in other media—in two pairs of porcelain and metal chandeliers and candlesticks, console tables, and ceramic wares brought from the nearby villa in which Margaret Abegg lived until three years ago. Whereas the three chasubles in the preceding room

Figure 3
Eighteenth-Century Silk. Reproduced with permission of The Abegg-Stiftung. Photographer: Christoph von Virag.

were as flat as the wall hangings (Cat. nos 7, 41, 131), the sack back dress (Cat. no. 185) that appeared to mount a couple of steps towards an impressive backdrop of silk conveyed the way in which textile design determined the cut of dress in this period. Falling simply in pleats from the neckline, the back of the *robe à la française*, with its wide skirts worn over hoops (*panniers*), was the perfect shape and size to parade the design. The textile mattered infinitely more than the cut in the mid-eighteenth century, as seasonal changes in the patterns on silks offered clues as to the wearer's social status and taste—for those in the know, at any rate (Ribeiro 1984; Thornton 1965). The refashioning of dress was not unusual, however, due to the value of the textiles, and this particular sack reinforced the recurring *leitmotiv* of recycling: its body conformed to 1730s cut, its sleeves had been remodeled in the 1750s or 1760s, just as such silks began to fall from fashion.

Two particular subsections within the exhibition underline the critical thinking and original research behind the whole enterprise. The section devoted to design explained clearly how specially trained designers conceived their patterns in the form of watercolors on paper, and juxtaposed silks in the Abegg-Stiftung's own collection with photographs of surviving designs from public collections in Paris and Lyons (Cat. nos 131, 132, 134, 137). The matching of silks with original design work is not as easy as it sounds, as complete design repeats for a given fabric do not seem to survive. Thus, the task comprises the rather painstaking identification of an element or motif in a fabric. It is complicated by the fact that designs on paper do not look the same as designs in the fabric because metallic yarns have to be conveyed in gouache (a color rather than gold or silver). Moreover, the background of the textile is often textured, while that of the paper is plain. The designs that the curator of the exhibition, Anna Jolly, discovered were amongst those that defined the exhibition title, as they combined fantastic architectural features (for example, landscapes seen through windows) with flowers, silver vessels, fans, Chinese lanterns, dogs frolicking by fountains, and birds bathing in them. Sadly, the technicalities of transferring these freehand designs into woven form did not receive any attention, no doubt because the technical point papers have disappeared. A further, rather nice touch in this section was the inclusion of designs that derived from existing fabrics, drawn at a later date, probably for the purposes of reproduction—another salutory warning about recycling and the difficulties of identifying original eighteenth-century silks (Cat. no. 139). The section on monochrome textiles was bold in a rather different way—it included an example of a silk for which the manufacturer/weaver had miscalculated the weight of the brocading wefts relative to the ground weave (Cat. no. 70). The heavy rustic scene in different shades of brown chenille has made the acid yellow *cannetillé* ground buckle. Here again was a salutory lesson, for seldom are mistakes in weaving chosen for exhibition although there are plenty of references in commercial correspondence of the period to clients' lack of satisfaction with what they received and their demands for mollification—often in the form of a renegotiated price (Coural 1988: 99).

While much could be gained purely from visual inspection of the exhibits, an appreciation of the informative supporting text panels and labels would have been much affected by the linguistic ability of visitors. Irredeemably monolingual anglophones had access to the overarching themes of the different sections through the brochure available on entry, and are lucky that the catalog raisonné carries a translation of its German introduction and an explanation of the headings used for each catalog entry. The latter was perhaps not a text to read during a short visit, but undoubtedly deserves further consultation for the lucidity of the discursive section, which fills many of the gaps considered too detailed for the general public, and because of the meticulous descriptions of each of the Abegg's naturalistic silks (194 eighteenth-century originals, and sixteen nineteenth- and twentieth-century versions). Sadly, at 280 Swiss francs (£125/US$200), it will only be within the means of a few specialist libraries where it will act as an excellent research tool for future students of eighteenth-century silks, and not only those of this restricted period. Its greatest strengths, from a historian's point of view, lie in its willingness to demystify the process of identification and attribution of eighteenth-century silks, and to indicate that it is impossible to be confident about the geographical origins of silks without prior knowledge of their provenance or dated documents associated with them. This essay relays the research resources (primary and secondary) on which judgments have been based, whether textual, visual (preparatory design drawings) or material (comparable dated textile "documents") and discusses critically the dangers of using guild regulations on widths and the number of warp and weft threads per width therein. Sections on the use and reuse of silks and on nineteenth-century imitations and reproductions are also very helpful in underlining the complexities of the subject. For art historians interested in the appearance of silks and their relationship to other decorative objects, the sections on eighteenth-century views of art and nature, the development of naturalism in silk design in France and other European countries, and in other decorative arts offer a useful overview of the subject, and include some rather nicely chosen examples. Technical weaving data are included in a final section which makes sense of the very specific terminology used to define each piece in both the exhibition and the catalog. An excellent bibliography, especially with regard to exhibition catalogs, complements the publication.

Happily, *Of Gardens and Castles* will have a life beyond the exhibition thanks to Anna Jolly's splendid catalog. However, for all that its photographs are excellent, they do not conjure up the sheer sensual pleasure of contact with the textiles themselves. The silks glowed with vigor despite their age, demonstrating the skills and imagination of their makers, and suggesting their desirability as prized possessions of an aristocratic elite. The fact that they did this so eloquently is a tribute to the way in which they were selected and displayed.

References

Ackermann, Hans Christoph. 2000. *Seidengewebe des 18. Jahrhunderts, vol. 1, Bizarre Seiden*. Riggisberg: Abegg-Stiftung.

AML (Archives muncipales de Lyon), 1758. CC178 *Rolle de capitation*. Grande Fabrique, 1758–9.

Coural, Chantal. 1988. *Soieries de Lyon. Commandes Royales au XVIIIe siècle*. Lyon: Musée des Tissus.

Jolly, Anna. 2002. *Seidengewebe des 18. Jahrhunderts, vol. II. Naturalismus*. Riggisberg: Abegg-Stiftung.

Poni, Carlo. 1997. "Fashion as Flexible Production: The Strategies of the Lyon Silk Merchants in the Eighteenth Century" in C. F. Sabel and J. Zeitlin (eds), *World of Possibilities: Flexibility and Mass Production in Western Industrialization*, pp. 37–74. Cambridge: Cambridge University Press.

Ribeiro, Aileen. 1984. *Dress in Eighteenth Century Europe 1715–1789*. London: Batsford.

Rothstein, Natalie. 1998. *Flowers-Blumen-Fleurs, English 18th-Century Silks*. Riggisberg: Abegg-Stiftung.

Thornton, Peter. 1965. *Baroque and Rococo Silks*. London: Faber & Faber.

Book Review

Weaving the Word: The Metaphorics of Weaving and Female Textual Production
Kathryn Sullivan Kruger.

Architecture and the Text: The (S)crypts of Joyce and Piranesi
Jennifer Bloomer.

Book Review

Weaving the Word: The Metaphorics of Weaving and Female Textual Production (Selinsgrove: Susquehanna University Press and London: Associated University Press, 2001) by Kathryn Sullivan Kruger.

Architecture and the Text: The (S)crypts of Joyce and Piranesi (New Haven and London: Yale University Press, 1993) by Jennifer Bloomer.

Apart from pockets of thinking that consider the crafts theoretically impenetrable because of their foundation in tactile rather than intellectual knowledge, interdisciplinary research is paying increasing attention to the comparative opportunities textiles offer. In particular, analysis of the similarities between texts and textiles is one of the many areas expanding under this broadened field of vision. Writing and woven textiles, in particular, lend themselves to comparison on many levels, from the linguistic roots the two words share, to the structural similarities found in networks of words and threads. Kathryn Sullivan Kruger's *Weaving the Word: The Metaphorics of Weaving and Female Textual Production* (2001) and Jennifer Bloomer's *Architecture and the Text: The (S)crypts of Joyce and Piranesi* (1993) address this particular interdisciplinary comparison through two distinct styles.

Kruger frames her study by arguing that the communicative role textiles have long played warrants their addition to the literary lexicon as examples of some of the earliest "texts." Kruger believes that initially story telling and weaving were analogous acts. Departing from these tangible examples, Kruger then moves to develop Kristeva's concept of the Maternal Mother (textile) from which the infant (text) issues forth. From this framework, she analyzes four Greek myths, William Blake's *The Four Zoas* and paintings that depict Lord Alfred Tennyson's *Lady of Shalott*. Kristeva's early theory is explained to be the "metaphoric net" through which these subsequent examples are captured although there are moments when the theory is less engaged. Nonetheless, the variety of early sources Kruger draws upon does support her assertion that textiles have carried the honor, and burden, of story telling long before woman or man put pen to paper.

Textile, Volume 1, Issue 1, pp. 107–109
Reprints available directly from the Publishers.
Photocopying permitted by licence only.
© 2003 Berg. Printed in the United Kingdom.

REVIEWED BY JESSICA HEMMINGS

A further interdisciplinary twist is presented in chapter five when Kruger compares depictions of literature's *Lady of Shalott* rendered in paint. Ironically this step draws Kruger back into more concrete territory with analysis settling around the manner in which the transition from paper to paint altered initial authorial intent. What Kruger does not construct herself, and it is a tempting possibility, is an overtly "woven" text. This structural technique can build a literal example of the comparison at hand although there is a risk that the results will feel as though they are slavishly reliant on a formula. Jennifer Bloomer's *Architecture and the Text: The (S)crypts of Joyce and Piranesi* (1993) avoids these pitfalls through its ability to present a woven text that addresses her observations, both literal and metaphoric, on the nature of writing and architecture. For her sources she draws on James Joyce's *Finnegans Wake* and the drawings of Piranesi, two artists she explains have haunted and, one must assume, inspired her to embark on the task of delineating the connections that make a simultaneous study of the two valuable.

Bloomer's text takes on a far more experimental form, with a series of key words such as "mapping" and "weaving" set in brackets throughout the text. In the introduction, Bloomer encourages alternate readings of the text determined by markers other than sequential turning of numbered pages. The system of brackets offers one such opportunity by visually linking passages that incorporate like terms. The "threads" that result can be followed from beginning to end, and across the knots and frays that inevitably arise. As a result, Bloomer's study looks less at the metaphors weaving and writing share than in inherent structural commonalities.

The works of Kruger and Bloomer, like all interdisciplinary studies, can be read on two levels. One level is for those of us unfamiliar with the specific examples who must instead satisfy ourselves with a reading of the manner in which the comparison came about. The other is for the well read, or the lucky, who find themselves familiar with the specific examples at hand and are able to enjoy both the manner of comparison and are able to address the examples in detail. While interdisciplinary comparisons of textiles and texts will inevitably draw reference from sources of enormous cultural and chronological breadth this should certainly not be seen as a deterrent for future scholars and readers. For what makes these studies ring true in so many ears is the breadth of connections under investigation as well as the infinite comparisons still waiting to be assembled.

Book Review

The Devil's Cloth: A History of Stripes and Striped Fabric
Michel Pastoureau

Book Review

The Devil's Cloth: A History of Stripes and Striped Fabric by Michel Pastoureau (Columbia University Press, 2001). Part of the European Perspectives. A series in Social Thought and Cultural Criticism edited by Lawrence D. Kritzman. Translated by Jody Gladding.

This is by turns a charming, inspiring and engagingly eccentric book. As the author explains in his preface, it is a text he felt impelled to write, not one that was commissioned. It developed from his observations early in his researches into medieval art, that striped clothing often marks out negative characters.

Subsequent work led him later into the middle ages and way beyond, as the lively narrative pursues the shifting meanings through the centuries, of stripes on cloth, clothing and other surfaces. From the pejorative stripe to the good stripe, the aristocratic stripe, the romantic stripe, the revolutionary stripe, the artist's stripe, the athletic stripe and stripe phobia, he leads the story thematically, shifting stripe-like between history and speculation, to consider subjects from servants' livery to prison uniform, bathing suits to flags, and then onto all kinds of other semiotic arenas: animal coats, wallpaper, toothpaste and pedestrian crossings. It is in discussion of the last of these that the author shows some of his questing interpretation skills to best effect:

Stripes on the ground indicate both passage and the difficulty of passage. Alternating empty zones and full zones, they require obedience and precaution, as if there were some danger of falling into the spaces separating the white bands. Here again it is a matter of a filter, letting the pedestrian's legs pass, but retaining all his attention.

The stripe, he maintains, is a cultural mark, representing an opposition to, or imposition upon, nature. A striped surface implies the desire to contain something ambivalent, indistinct and uncontrollable. Hence its use in prison uniforms, or in lunatic asylums as a means of signalling control. However, while he is alert to double and shifting meanings, at times, Pastoureau's argument is overly deterministic. For example, he asserts that in the animal world striped pelts are to be admired for

Textile, Volume 1, Issue 1, pp. 111–112
Reprints available directly from the Publishers.
Photocopying permitted by licence only.
© 2003 Berg. Printed in the United Kingdom.

their precision or to be feared for their predatory associations. But there is another story to be told about camouflage and evasion. Though he is often sensitive to the dual character of the stripe, he gives much less attention to its self-effacing nature, than to its ostentation.

Pastoureau is a medievalist and ironically, it is with the medieval material that he is least flexible. The pejorative story of medieval stripes hinges around a scandal in thirteenth-century Paris over the striped habits of Carmelite friars. So much were they ridiculed and associated with untrustworthiness, it led eventually in 1295 to a ban on striped vestments by Papal bull. It is a fascinating and significant episode and Pastoureau goes on to refer to a number of other condemnations of striped cloth for clerics and to give many interesting examples of stripes, which appear to signal unworthy character. Much as one would hope and wish that he was right, historical interpretations cannot always be so neatly licked into shape and there are dangers in assuming that his interpretation of "the devil's cloth" from thirteenth-century France applies universally in the Middle Ages. At the risk of spoiling the story, there are many famous examples of non-transgressive stripes. There are the royal vestments from thirteenth-century Spain, which survive at the convent of Las Huelgas in Burgos, a number of which are gorgeously striped. From the excavations of the city of London have come quantities of striped cloths: they were

evidently part of normal daily attire. Clearly from the opposite of the devil's realm, there survives in the Bavarian National Museum in Munich a small fourteenth-century Swiss tapestry, showing two angels in vertically striped vestments holding heraldic shields. And so on.

One of the most problematic areas is his own specialist field, heraldry. He explains that the striped blazons that abound among perfectly worthy families have no symbolic meaning, whereas there are also abundant examples of fictitious bad characters who are given stripes. But how could viewers be expected to keep the distinction clear between good stripes and bad ones? If stripes in heraldry or in any other aristocratic accoutrements really signalled bad character, then surely they would have been just as avidly avoided as were the devil's horns and forked tail. In the end, Pastoureau weakens his argument by overstating the case. Accepting that there might be a wider range both of stripes and their interpretation in the Middle Ages, could only have enriched the foundations of his story.

This is such a thought-provoking book, written with such conviction, that these seem like nit-picking criticisms. But it is important to note that this is more of an ideas book than a history book. It is a book about visual culture in the Roland Barthes school. Its major contribution is that it draws attention to a whole range of interesting questions and gets more mileage from the stripe than ever before.

Notes for Contributors

Articles should be approximately 25 pages in length and *must* include a three-sentence biography of the author(s). Interviews should not exceed 15 pages and do not require an author biography. Exhibition and book reviews are normally 500 to 2,000 words in length. The Publishers will require a disk as well as a hard copy of any contributions (please mark clearly on the disk what word-processing program has been used). Berg accepts most programs with the exception of Clarisworks.

Textile: The Journal of Cloth & Culture will produce one issue a year devoted to a single topic. Persons wishing to organize a topical issue are invited to submit a proposal which contains a hundred-word description of the topic together with a list of potential contributors and paper subjects. Proposals are accepted only after review by the journal editors and in-house editorial staff at Berg Publishers.

Manuscripts

Manuscripts with disks should be submitted to: *Textile: The Journal of Cloth & Culture*. Manuscripts will be acknowledged by the editor and entered into the review process discussed below. Manuscripts without illustrations will not be returned unless the author provides a self-addressed stamped envelope. Submission of a manuscript to the journal will be taken to imply that it is not being considered elsewhere for publication, and that if accepted for publication, it will not be published elsewhere, in the same form, in any language, without the consent of the editor and publisher. It is a condition of acceptance by the editor of a manuscript for publication that the publishers automatically acquire the copyright of the published article throughout the world. *Textile: The Journal of Cloth & Culture* does not pay authors for their manuscripts nor does it provide retyping, drawing, or mounting of illustrations.

Style

U.S. spelling and mechanicals are to be used. Authors are advised to consult *The Chicago Manual of Style (14th Edition)* as a guideline for style. *Webster's Dictionary* is our arbiter of spelling. We encourage the use of major subheadings and, where appropriate, second-level subheadings. Manuscripts submitted for consideration as an article must contain: a title page with the full title of the article, the author(s) name and address, a three-sentence biography for each author, and a 200 word abstract. Do not place the author's name on any other page of the manuscript.

Manuscript Preparation

Manuscripts must be typed double-spaced (including quotations, notes, and references cited), one side only, with at least one-inch margins on standard paper using a typeface no smaller than 12pts. The original manuscript and a copy of the text on disk *(please ensure it is clearly marked with the word-processing program that has been used) must* be submitted, along with black and white *original* photographs (to be returned). Authors should retain a copy for their records. Any necessary artwork *must* be submitted with the manuscript.

Footnotes

Footnotes appear as "Notes" at the end of articles. Authors are advised to include footnote material in the text whenever possible. Notes are to be numbered consecutively throughout the paper and are to be typed double-spaced at the end of the text. (Do not use any footnoting or end-noting programs which your software may offer as this text becomes irretrievably lost at the typesetting stage.)

References

The list of references should be limited to, and inclusive of, those publications actually cited in the text. References are to be cited in the body of the text in parentheses with author's last name, the year of original publication, and page number—e.g., (Rouch 1958: 45). Titles and publication information appear as "References" at the end of the article and should be listed alphabetically by author and chronologically for each author. Names of journals and publications should appear in full. Film and video information appears as "Filmography". References cited should be typed double-spaced on a separate page. *References not presented in the style required will be returned to the author for revision.*

Tables

All tabular material should be part of a separately numbered series of "Tables." Each table must be typed on a separate sheet and identified by a short descriptive title. Footnotes for tables appear at the bottom of the table. Marginal notations on manuscripts should indicate approximately where tables are to appear.

Figures

All illustrative material (drawings, maps, diagrams, and photographs) should be designated "Figures." They must be submitted in a form suitable for publication without redrawing. Drawings should be carefully done with black ink on either hard, white, smooth-surfaced board or good quality tracing paper. Ordinarily, computer-generated drawings are not of publishable quality. Color photographs are encouraged by the publishers. Whenever possible, photographs should be 8 × 10 inches. The publishers encourage artwork to be submitted as scanned files (300 dpi or above) on disk or via email. All figures should be clearly numbered on the back and numbered consecutively. All captions should be typed double-spaced on a separate page. Marginal notations on manuscripts should indicate approximately where figures are to appear. While the editors and publishers will use ordinary care in protecting all figures submitted, they cannot assume responsibility for their loss or damage. Authors are discouraged from submitting rare or non-replaceable materials. It is the author's responsibility to secure written copyright clearance on *all* photographs and drawings that are not in the public domain. Copyright should be obtained for worldwide rights and on-line publishing.

Criteria for Evaluation

Textile: The Journal of Cloth & Culture is a refereed journal. Manuscripts will be accepted only after review by both the editors and anonymous reviewers deemed competent to make professional judgments concerning the quality of the manuscript. Upon request, authors will receive reviewers' evaluations.

Reprints for Authors

Twenty-five reprints of authors' articles will be provided to the first named author free of charge. Additional reprints may be purchased upon request.